open
your
eyes

EXTRAORDINARY EXPERIENCES
IN FARAWAY PLACES

edited by
JILL DAVIS

VIKING

*This book is for all of the wonderful people
we met in faraway places*

VIKING
Published by Penguin Group
Penguin Young Readers Group, 345 Hudson Street, New York, New York 10014, U.S.A.
Published in 2003 by Viking, a division of Penguin Young Readers Group

1 3 5 7 9 10 8 6 4 2

Introduction copyright © Jill Davis, 2003
Empress copyright © Lois Lowry, 2003
Simunye copyright © Piper Dellums, 2003
Little American Mom, Big French Suitcase copyright © Susie Morgenstern, 2003
Join the Army and See the World copyright © Harry Mazer, 2003
An Innocent Abroad copyright © Minna Murra, 2003
Looking for America copyright © Elizabeth Partridge, 2003
A Brief Guide to the Ghosts of Great Britain copyright © M. T. Anderson, 2003
Ahoy, Down There! copyright © Graham Salisbury, 2003
MK copyright © Jean Fritz, 2003
The Girl Who Had No Story and Had to Steal One copyright © Kathleen Krull
& Jacqueline Brewer, 2003
All rights reserved

LIBRARY OF CONGRESS CATALOGING-IN-PUBLICATION DATA
Open your eyes : extraordinary experiences in far away places / edited
by Jill Davis.
p.   cm.
Summary: A collection of memoirs and stories about a variety of travel
experiences that changed the lives of some of today's most popular
writers, including Lois Lowry, Susie Morgenstern, and Harry Mazer.
ISBN 0-670-03616-1 (hardcover)
1. Voyages and travels—Anecdotes—Juvenile literature. [1. Voyages
and travels—Anecdotes. 2. Authors, American.] I. Davis, Jill.
G133.O64 2003   2003010100

Printed in U.S.A.
Set in Sabon
Book design by Teresa Kietlinski

Special thanks to Melanie Cecka, Catherine Frank, Tracy Gates, Anne Rivers Gunton,
Regina Hayes, Teresa Kietlinski, Ellen Levine, and Janet Pascal.

contents

"Travel is fatal to prejudice, bigotry and narrow-mindedness."

—Mark Twain

introduction
by JILL DAVIS

WHEN I THINK about it, few things that happened in my childhood suggested to me that one day there would be more to experience than life in my own small town. Of course I always knew I'd be going to college. But that was the future and I couldn't even imagine it.

And then high school came, and in my junior year something unexpected happened.

France.

France came to me in the form of an eleventh-grade exchange student. Her name was Catherine (pronounced CaTREEN), and we got to be friends. My first thought when I saw this exotic-looking girl sitting in the back of French class was, *Five days in the same outfit? Does this girl never change?* But underneath it, my brain was bubbling over and giving birth to curiosity. In those first days, I remember thinking, *I don't know a thing about France, but this certainly wasn't what I expected.* Despite my fear of her alternative hygiene, we became fast friends. The friendship led to my first trip outside the United States, to L'Aiguillon-sur-Mer on the west coast of her country, directly on the other side of the Atlantic Ocean, and just down from England. That trip was the one that changed my life. It was the beginning of my fascination with France—and a lifelong friendship with Catherine.

For me, July 1984 was filled with intimidating shell-fish, translations of French conversation, and a host of the most exotic teenagers I could never have imagined. Christophe and Valérie were the beautiful couple. He was light-brown skinned with a long Roman nose. She was sexy in a way I had never seen in the United States. Their beauty was so natural, so different from the current style at home—big hair and the Madonna belt-and-earrings craze. Valérie's sister, Pascale, was kind of earthy but mysterious, and also very beautiful. It wasn't unusual to see Pascale sitting poolside topless. She was coupled with a short black guy named Harold, who dressed only in the colors of Jamaica—red, yellow, and green—and always joked with me, half-nice and half-mean. And to them, I was exotic—the American. What had they always thought an American would look like? Act like? They only knew us from movies and TV. However curious I was about all of them, they seemed equally interested in me.

Now, almost twenty years later, it really does seem like a dream. At the crêperie: eating crêpes with banana and chocolate and drinking hard cider in wooden bowls. Or at the bar, La Paloma: sitting packed at long tables with every kind of person—

smoking, eating, drinking, talking, hearing Bob Marley on the jukebox—all having the time of our lives. It was exponentially more fun than anything I had ever experienced at home. Everything just seemed to *mean* so much more. I remember a motorcycle ride to a nightclub, called a *bôite*, where teenagers danced their hearts out and stayed till dawn. I remember learning how to sing French children's songs from some of the boys and spending my time trying to remember them as we walked around the carnival rides which lived in L'Aiguillon for the whole summer. And I remember looking into the eyes of my new friends and seeing something I had never seen before. Maybe it was openness, honesty. Or maybe I was just looking too hard. Maybe I saw myself through their eyes, and I noticed I was different in France. That I liked myself a little bit more. Or perhaps it was just the magic of a teenage summer.

At home I would have been driving around from movie theater to pancake house with the same old gang of suburban sixteen-year-olds. By contrast, Catherine's friends ranged in age from twelve to twenty, and none of them even seemed to have parents. In L'Aiguillon, there were no phone calls needed to make plans—just get up, get dressed, and walk toward the beach and find people. They were always around, playing pool, having a drink, listening to music near the ocean. . . .

✶ ✶ ✶ ✶

When I came home, I knew a lot of new things. I knew different music. I knew interracial couples. I knew all about the west coast of France. I knew that swimming topless at the beach wasn't a big deal. I had seen how meals were savored—punctuated with little yogurts and cheeses for dessert—and salad! always *after* the meal. I knew that life was fun and interesting. I felt older, and clued-in, and a part of a world that would remain there across the ocean, despite my absence from it.

Two years later I was at UMass Amherst, and two years after that, back in France. This time I wasn't living with a French family and being shown around by Catherine. Now I was on my own, part of an exchange group from UMass Boston, and living in a huge Paris apartment with an old widow.

As a new resident of Madame Morizet's home, I wasn't sure what the rules were. The adventures were coming fast and furious, because I had so much to learn about living in Paris. Some lessons were learned in the apartment. For example Madame Morizet's tradition each evening was to watch the French news in her dimly lit spare bedroom, correcting the grammar of the French president, François Mitterand. (I joined her now and again and noted her intensity. But my French wasn't good, so I could scarcely laugh along.) This, to me, was a lesson in French culture. Some of my other adventures took place outside the apartment. One in particular comes to mind.

Late fall 1987, I had a visitor, another UMass student and a friend of my brother. Her name was Carrie. She camped out with me, *chez* Madame Morizet, for a day or two, and then planned to go on to Switzerland. When it came time for her to go, I said I'd take her to the train. *Au revoir, Madame Morizet. A bientôt!* Saying good-bye always made me feel like someone cared about me when I was so far from home.

At the train station, I decided to help Carrie with her bag. Up the steps we climbed onto the train heading north and east to Switzerland. I must have been looking around the train when I realized it was moving. The doors all simultaneously closed and locked, and when I looked out the window I saw that we were leaving the station.

I shrieked to the ticket man, "Wait! I'm not going!" *Attendez! Je n'y vais pas!* I felt my stomach fall down to my feet. I must have turned white, but Carrie was the one who really looked scared. Actually, I was more excited than scared. I started thinking: *Can I go?* I took inventory of myself. And then, *Oh no! I don't even have my passport with me. That means I really can't go. No money, either! I am a stowaway!*

I had the feeling that what was happening to me was my biggest adventure yet. In my whole life! This was the definition of independence. Twenty years old and caught on a train from Paris to Switzerland. No one in the whole world knows where I am! But soon the thrill was gone. I learned that I was going to be forced off at the next stop. So I asked, *"C'est où, le premier arrêt?"* Where is the first stop?

"Trois!" he said, and showed me a train schedule and pointed to a word that said Troyes. Oh. Troyes. Also pronounced *trwa*, just like *trois*, the number three in French. And it was almost two hours outside Paris.

"What will I do?" I asked anyone and no one and everyone around me. The train seats were not set up in rows of two like on Amtrak, but in little sections in which three or four people faced each other and could close the compartment door. I sat down in the same section as Carrie. Looking at her, I began to see that my little adventure was disrupting her big plan. I'd just have to go home.

Next I found out something even worse. The first train back from Troyes to Paris would be "At five in zee morning, tomorrow," according to the youthful and completely unsympathetic ticket collector. No problem. I would arrive at the train station around eleven P.M. and just hang out there by myself for six hours. What would I eat? Where would I sleep? On a hard wooden bench? What if the station was cold or was just an outdoor kiosk? What if I got attacked or abducted? For now, I had company, but what would the station be like? How could Carrie just abandon me? Why didn't I have my money?

Two hours. Two hours. Two hours.

That's when I heard a shy voice.

"Excuse me, mademoiselle." I looked over toward the window and saw a young dark-haired woman. "I live in Troyes. And you will come to stay with me, with my family."

Writing this now, I honestly don't remember if she said this in French or in English. It could have been Swahili for all I cared. She was an angel.

When we finally arrived in Troyes, there were her parents waiting for her and as it turned out, me, too. They were pleased to meet the lost American student.

Their kindness was truly immeasurable. I just couldn't imagine this happening back home, where we don't tend to invite complete strangers to sleep over. Yet I hope I would do the same for a lost foreigner. I found out that the family name was Berger. A mom, a dad, the grown daughter, and her tiny little daughter named Cappucine. No sign of a dad for Cappucine. I was taking in more about French culture.

"You will have some hot chocolate and go to bed," said Madame Berger to me, her newly adopted refugee.

"Come down to the basement and let me show you something," said the kindly Monsieur Berger, as he led me down some carpeted steps. And there in the cozy little basement in Troyes, hanging on the wall, was a collection of license plates from all over the United States. "You see," he said with a big grin, "these are all of the places I want to visit in America!" I still remember he had a big radio on a platform next to them, where he probably tuned in to the news from around the world.

Back in their airy suburban kitchen, the family gathered around the table to tell me a little bit about the small city of Troyes, once a medieval village and recently restored. "We will take you on a tour tomorrow morning before the train," said Madame Berger, and tucked me into a mattress on the living room floor. I went to sleep with the taste of hot chocolate in my mouth and thoughts of castles and walled cities in my head. I hadn't called Madame Morizet. I hoped she would have gone to bed early and not noticed I was missing. This would surely be the last year she'd host a troublesome American!

I don't remember the train ride back to Paris, though the tour of the town of Troyes was cool. Actually, it felt good to be out of the city, if only for twelve hours. The mishap sort of opened my eyes. Within the space of a few hours I went to opposite extremes: from embarking on an exciting and exhilarating adventure to being rescued from what could have been a dangerous situation. I was eager to get home and assure my worried widow that I was fine.

But looking back, the most surprising memory of

the whole trip was probably what Madame Morizet said to me when I arrived home. She said, "*Bonjour, Jill.*" She hadn't even noticed I was gone.

✶ ✶ ✶ ✶

The events in these stories have helped to shape my life. The summer in L'Aiguillon-sur-Mer ignited my love for living in France and for French people and their culture; the year in Paris was when I grew into an adult. I wondered how traveling to faraway places made other people see themselves and their worlds differently. I wanted to know whether others felt, as I did, that stories are the best souvenirs of all. I wanted to hear their stories.

In *Open Your Eyes*, ten writers will be your guides to some of the experiences that changed their lives: a boarding school in England; parenthood in France; the most beautiful spots in Italy; China on the Yangtze; a tiny shop in Tokyo, Japan; places inside the United States that sometimes felt like a foreign country; and even Plzen, Czechoslovakia, as World War II is ending. Thank you to the writers for sharing their extraordinary experiences.

Here I am, twelve years old, Christmas day in Tokyo in 1948. It was the family maids, Teruko-San and Ritsuko-San, who dressed me and tied my obi.

empress
by LOIS LOWRY

"SHE'S IN NO danger from the Japanese." I overheard my father say that. Then Mother replied, but her voice was a murmur that I could only partly make out. Their door was closed.

I knew she had complained to him that I'd been running off. Not running, really. Biking. Back home in Pennsylvania, not that long before, I had navigated the streets of my small town a hundred times— a thousand—no, maybe a *million* times, on my bike, and Mother had never minded. As long as I was home by dinnertime; that was the unwritten rule.

But now I lived in Tokyo, and Tokyo was different, Mother was pointing out to Dad, and bigger, and . . . now I could hear her hesitate in her description as she continued to fret about me to my father. It was *foreign*, I knew she was thinking, but Mother would be aware how foolish it would sound to call it that.

"She's only eleven," she said, finally, "and very *trusting*."

"You should be, too," he replied.

↙ ↙ ↙ ↙

She was right, of course: Tokyo was different, and bigger. Much, much bigger. My Pennsylvania town would fit into a tiny part of it, into a neighborhood. Answering Mother's worries in my mind, I thought: All I'm doing is riding around my neighborhood the way I always have.

It was just that the neighborhood, the neighborhood known as Shibuya, seemed so strange to Mother. Mother was scared of Tokyo.

Dad wasn't. He'd been here two years already. A career army officer, he had entered Japan immediately after the war ended, after the bomb destroyed Hiroshima. We had waited at home, writing letters to him, until finally he said it was time. Men came and packed our things. My sister, fourteen, wept dramatically and said lengthy good-byes to her many friends on the telephone. Not me. I was eager to be off, to see something new, to eat different food, learn new words in a foreign tongue. Though I knew I would be attending an international school, that my classes would be taught in English, and I would be wearing my usual uninteresting clothes—still, I hoped something exotic would happen to me. Nothing ever had. I feared that nothing ever would.

Now we were here, and our home was not particularly exotic at all. The government-issue furniture was sturdy and beige. There was never enough hot water. The books I had loved were all in storage in Pennsylvania, and there were none in the Tokyo house.

But we had a gardener and maids. The maids spoke poor English, though they tried hard, and giggled a lot. I eavesdropped on their rapid, unintelligible chatter. I watched the gardener leave in the evening, and wondered where he went when he disappeared beyond the gate, into the mass of hurrying Japanese. The world outside the quiet walled courtyard of our house was noisy, crowded, and filled with color, though it included rubble still, left from bombed buildings.

And it all made Mother nervous.

"Stay close to the house," she said, "and don't talk to anyone."

I scowled at her. "How can I talk to anyone? The only things I know how to say are yes, no, thank you, good morning, and maybe a few other things. I keep trying to get the cook to teach me more, but she just giggles."

My father tried once again to reassure her. "She's fine, Kate. The Japanese people *like* children. They're known for their kindness to children. All children. Even Americans."

Mother sighed.

My sister had made friends already. An American girl named Betsy lived nearby, a high school girl eager for information about movies back in the States. She and my sister had begun to pal around, talking in their mysterious teenage language, excluding me.

Mother had friends, too: wives of the men who worked with Dad. They played bridge in the afternoons at each other's houses while the men were at work. They shopped at the big military store called the Tokyo PX. Mother had bought a large many-drawered chest that she said was called a kitchen *tansu*, used for holding cooking and dining supplies in a Japanese home. It was not new. She called it an antique and thought she was lucky to have found it, but I wondered whose it had been, whether their house had been bombed, if this lovely piece of furniture had been lifted out of rubble. In our own Tokyo home she had placed it in the dining room and served hors d'oeuvres from it when she and Dad gave cocktail parties, as they did often. Cocktail parties were a way of life for my parents and their military friends; they instructed the cook to make tiny delicacies for guests to nibble as they sipped martinis.

I was eager for school to begin so that I could become part of a group, the way I had been back home in the States. But it hadn't happened yet. And in the meantime I had my bike. And I had the whole of *out there*, as my mother called it, somehow making the phrase sound vaguely sinister, waiting to be explored.

"Well, be careful. Promise." She acceded to my father, giving me permission to roam.

"*Hai*," I replied, using one of my few Japanese words, and saluted, a gesture that always made my father, the colonel, grin.

*   *   *   *

The smells were different from anything I knew. Not unpleasant, but different: smoky, fermented. Fishy. Indeed, in front of the open shops I could see baskets of dried fish, the papery silver faces staring up with glistening wide-open eyes. Dried grasshoppers, too, in baskets. People actually ate them. I imagined the crunch with a giddy shiver.

People jostled me as I made my way through the crowd. The only blonde in a sea of dark-haired humanity, I was self-conscious and yearned to blend in, to become part of the throng, less of an outsider. But it was impossible. I felt people touch my long hair surreptitiously and murmur.

I glanced back to keep my bearings. I was walking on this crowded street, because it was too hard to negotiate by bicycle through all the people. Women shopping, babies strapped to their backs, carried their purchases wrapped in the cloth called *furoshiki*. Children wore dark blue uniforms: it was not vacation for them; they took school very seriously here. An oxcart came through, loaded with vegetables, piles of the huge radishes called *daikon*.

I had left my bike by the gate of a temple and kept the temple as a landmark, looking back now and then to be certain that I could retrace my steps to return. Mother was right that I wouldn't have a clue how to ask directions, though I thought I could throw myself on the mercy of strangers by using sign language if I had to. The street had curved a little but I could still see the red gate and the metallic shine of my green bicycle

A shopkeeper called to me in words I didn't understand and pointed to his wares displayed on open tables: toys, mostly, and souvenirs. Bright colored baby rattles hung from the side posts and made hollow tinkling sounds when they were bumped by the crowds. I saw countless statues of a sheepishly grinning pregnant woman, with an inscription at the base: KILROY WAS HERE. Kilroy was the joke name that American soldiers called themselves, I knew. The tasteless little figure was embarrassing, I thought, but also stupid and unimportant. He had dolls, too: gaudy pink celluloid with an acrid smell and painted faces with large blue baby eyes. He pointed to them with a hopeful look, but I shook my head. They didn't interest me. I was too old for dolls.

The shopkeeper was old, thin, stooped, with wisps of gray hair and leathery wrinkled skin. He said something unintelligible, smiled (I saw missing teeth, gaps in his smile), and beckoned that I should follow him inside.

"*She's too trusting,*" I had heard Mother say of me. It wasn't true. I assessed everything, sometimes at agonizing length.

Enemy? I thought of every Japanese person. *Are we enemies still? Do you hate me, wish you could kill me?*

At first I had thought it of our maids, Teruko, Ritsuko, and Aiko, with their shy admiration of the American clothes in our closets, and their dubious curiosity about the food Mother asked them to cook. I wondered if they had had young fiancés or husbands taken from them by war. Cousins inciner-ated in Hiroshima, perhaps. Maybe they yearned to put poison into the food they served to us. But I listened to them chattering and laughing in the kitchen and decided that they were very much like my teenage sister and her friend Betsy: harmless, silly, sweet.

I considered the question now of the stooped old man who was inviting me to enter the dim interior of his shop. *Enemy?* He was too old to have fought my father and too fragile to do me any harm. And there was an imploring quality to him. He continued to point inside with an eager pride, and so I nodded, saying with the nod that I wanted to see what it was that he wanted to show me. He had slipped off his own straw sandals and was indicating that I should remove my shoes. The scuffed brown loafers that had been my school shoes in sixth grade—Mother said I would need something new when I entered seventh next month—slipped off easily, and in my two-tone green Girl Scout socks I followed him and we made our way around the display of cheap toys in the front.

Farther back, through a curtained doorway, we entered a small room with a *tatami* floor. The light was dim, and I waited, squinting, until my eyes adjusted. The old man who had guided me there now squatted beside me, and so I knelt next to him. His hair smelled strongly of a sweet oil. Smiling, he talked rapidly—I understood nothing—and gestured, and finally I could see, in the murky light of the small unwindowed room, glass cases that held his treasures, elegant posed figurines: emperor, empress, handmaidens, musicians, courtiers, and even furniture—tiny brass-handled chests and delicate carved tables. I leaned close to see the faces, the features painted delicately, the small red lips, the curved dark eyes, so different from the garish pink smirk and pale blue startled circles of the cheap celluloid Kewpies.

They weren't souvenirs or playthings. The dolls were so exquisite, each different, and there were so many of them, arranged on seven red-carpeted tiers with the royal couple at the top, that it was like being in a museum. He talked rapidly, pointing, and I realized he was describing the various dolls, their costumes, their roles in the emperor's court.

There were small tags visible, with prices written in yen: thousands, it appeared, maybe even millions, though I was not certain what that meant in American dollars. My own allowance was one dollar a week. Surely he knew that an eleven-year-old girl in scuffed shoes could not afford to buy these dolls. I wasn't even carrying a purse. I spread my hands in front of me, open, trying to indicate their total emptiness, my poverty, my undesirability as a customer.

He didn't seem to care.

Reassured that he understood I could not be a customer, that I was not there under false pretenses, I relaxed and leaned forward to see the dolls more clearly.

The shopkeeeper swept his hand through the air in front of the glass case, indicating the entire magnificent royal court. "*Hina,*" he said, as if explaining.

"*Hai,*" I said to the old man. Yes.

The empress was my favorite, though ordinarily, in books or movies, I identified with lower classes, with suffering and needy people. I liked paupers, never princes.

But the empress, seated before a golden screen, wearing an elaborate black wig and an intricate purple and gold headdress, had a sad look on her delicate painted face. Perhaps, I found myself thinking, she was not fond of the emperor seated on her right. Perhaps their children had met misfortune. Perhaps their country was at war against barbarians. And perhaps they were losing.

She held an open fan decorated with multicolored ribbons in her two slender porcelain hands. With only the slightest gesture she could have raised the fan and shielded her face. She could have hidden her shame, if that's what she felt, or her sadness.

But of course an empress wouldn't.

I had created all of this—the unhappy dynastic

marriage, the unfortunate children, the war-torn country, the humiliating defeat—in my mind while kneeling on the smooth *tatami* of the shadowed room in silence. Beside me the shopkeeper still squatted, looking at the dolls with a kind of dignified pride, thinking his own thoughts. Then, from behind another curtained doorway at the opposite end of the room from the shop, I could hear, suddenly, the sound of dishes and of someone moving around. A radio was turned on at low volume. The shopkeeper stirred himself and rose. He went to the doorway and spoke quietly to someone inside. Then he turned and beckoned to me.

When I joined him at the doorway, he held the curtain aside for me and I went into a small room with a wooden floor where an old woman was beginning to prepare a meal. A kind of stove sat on a table; it looked like what we had used at Girl Scout camp in the States, hardly more than a box of bent tin over some kind of burner that had not yet been ignited. The woman, an apron over her cotton kimono, stood at a makeshift sink under a single faucet. She was washing rice. When I entered she turned and bowed to me.

The two spoke to each other in soft, rapid Japanese. I recognized only the word *hina* and thought he must be telling her that he had shown me the dolls of the royal court. She smiled, nodding her head, and looked pleased. Her hair, gray like his, was thin and knotted at the back of her head.

While they talked to each other, I glanced around the tiny kitchen, half the size of mine at home. A shelf held soap and a few cans of food as well as the small radio that continued to play a kind of repetitive music. There was no refrigerator, I noticed with surprise. But perhaps none was necessary. She was preparing rice, and a vegetable of some sort lay on the table beside the small stove, but there was no other food in sight.

There was no *tansu* with brass-handled drawers. Instead, in the corner, neatly stacked, I saw a pile of what looked like threadbare quilts.

I realized, suddenly, that this small, shabby room was their home. The quilts would be unrolled at night, the table moved to the side, and the old couple would sleep on this splintery floor.

I wondered if it had always been so.

They finished their conversation and turned back to me. I understood that it was time to leave. Politely the woman and I bowed to each other. I had been taught, as a small child, to curtsey after my Sunday School recitation. But I had never bowed. Yet here in this setting, it came naturally and felt right to lean forward slightly as a gesture of courtesy and respect.

When I looked at her face in order to say good-bye,

I saw that although her skin, like the shopkeeper's, was wrinkled and discolored, her features were as refined as those on the doll in the next room. She had the same straight nose, the same small mouth. As she watched me try awkwardly to express my friendship and thanks, she made no reply. But her eyes had the same look of proud sadness that I had seen on the porcelain empress.

Then she turned away and went back to the small container of rice and the cold water faucet.

The old man followed me through the room that held his treasured dolls and toward the front of the shop. He waited while I slipped my shoes back on. For the first time I realized that I was taller than he.

"Thank you," I said to him, as I turned to leave, "for showing me the *hina*."

But he wasn't listening. He had leaned down behind the table stacked with Kewpies and was fumbling with some boxes there. Then he stood and pressed something into my hand. A fan. I looked at it, puzzled at first, and then in delight I opened its bamboo folds until the stiffened paper revealed a design of flowering trees.

His head bobbed with pleasure. "*Sakura*," he said, and pointed to the design. Cherry blossoms.

We looked at the little painting together for a moment. Then reluctantly I refolded the fan and tried to return it to him. But his hands remained at his sides, and he bowed slightly. "*Dozo,*" he said.

"I don't have any money," I whispered apologetically. I patted my pockets, looking disappointed, trying to show how empty and flat they were, how devoid of any yen at all. Desperately I tried to remember some of the phrases my father had been trying to teach me. "*Sumimasen,*" I told the shopkeeper, and thrust the fan back toward him. I'm sorry.

But again he refused to accept it. Again he bowed.

Finally I bowed, mumbled a shy, "*Arigato gozaimasu. Sayonara,*" and left his shop, carrying the gift folded in my hand. I spotted the red gate of the temple ahead at the curve of the road and could see the shiny green of my bike leaning undisturbed against the wall. The crowds of passersby closed around me and a woman touched my hair. I heard her murmur, "*Kirei.*"

Pretty.

Carefully I unfolded my fan. I held it in front of my flat eleven-year-old chest so that its edge was level with the top button of my pink cotton blouse. The empress had held her fan at that height, so that its golden border met the deep vee where her alabaster neck disappeared into the fold of her kimono.

I tried to feel pretty, and failed. Instead, I felt too tall, too blonde, too American. I felt ashamed. But I made my face into the face of an empress, a face that pretended not to care. Then I walked on, holding my fan.

lois lowry

LOIS LOWRY feels her luck began with her birth order: the middle child of three. "That left me in between, and exactly where I wanted most to be: on my own," she explains. In her solitude, Lowry "lived in the world of books and [her] own vivid imagination."

With family members in the military Lowry has lived in many different places during her childhood and adult life: Hawaii, New York, Pennsylvania, Japan, Rhode Island, California, Connecticut, Florida, South Carolina, Massachusetts, and Maine. She is now settled back in Massachusetts, "living and writing in a house dominated by a very shaggy Tibetan Terrier named Bandit," with a second home in Maine.

Having twice won the Newbery Medal (for *Number the Stars* in 1990 and *The Giver* in 1994), Lowry is among the greats of children's literature. The circumstances of her second win were particularly unusual: "In 1994 [the Newbery Committee] couldn't find me. I was in Antarctica! Eventually they reached me by sending a radiogram. So I was feeling on top of the world, though, technically speaking, I was actually at the bottom."

Lowry's many books include the Anastasia series, the Sam series, and the Tate series, as well as a number of YA novels. Though her books vary in subject and technique, Lowry believes that "all of them deal, essentially, with the same general theme: the importance of human connections."

Reflecting on "Empress," Lowry says, "The time period contained in this story was probably no more than twenty minutes, and it happened over fifty years ago. But it seems like yesterday, because I was changed by it. Such small encounters—a brief meeting, a look exchanged, a tiny moment of surprise or pleasure—are the times I return to most often in my memory."

Lois Lowry has three grown children and four grandchildren.

Here we are at home in 1977 singing and dancing to "Greased Lightning."

simunye
by PIPER DELLUMS

I DON'T REMEMBER the name of the kid who drove us from Maryland to the mountains of Pennsylvania for a week of skiing, when I was twelve, only that he was my friend's older brother. What I do remember is sharing secrets about boys in pig-Latin with my very best friend Tina ("avid-Day orovitz-Hay is a otal-tay ox-fay"). I remember the fast-food stop we made somewhere after nightfall, and what happened in the parking lot as we were leaving.

"Hey you guys, look up ahead." He turned on the

van's high beams and pointed "It's hard to see them in the dark unless they are smiling . . . three coons waiting to be run over!" He took a sip of coffee and laughed.

"What's a coon?" Tina asked.

"Did you see how they froze in the headlights and scurried off like raccoons? Well, that's what they do," he said.

"Coons are spooks that only come out at night," his friend added from the front passenger seat.

The car filled with sudden laughter as the three young black men walked directly past the front of the van toward their parked car. They were clean-cut and handsome and reminded me of my brothers.

I felt sick to my stomach . . . afraid to breathe. I didn't want anyone to look at me, to notice that I too was black, a coon, a spook in the night.

Everyone in the back seat was staring at me now, whispering apologies through nervous crooked smiles. My lids were heavy holding back the pressure of shame. I wanted to get out of the car, out of my mind, and out of my skin. Tina put her hand on my shoulder.

"Don't worry, Piper," she said. "We don't think of you as being black."

I had always believed I would not feel this kind of pain because of how hard I tried to blend into our exclusive white community of Chevy Chase, Maryland. It was my role. In fact, I had been playing this role ever since third grade, when I had been told by my teacher that a dark-skinned girl couldn't play Snow White. From then on, I didn't connect with, relate to, or allow myself to be identified by anything that could be remotely considered ethnic; leaving me with a grave confusion that all but erased my identity. But another image haunted me that night in the van on the way to go skiing: I saw the *Life* magazine picture of three black men dangling by their necks at the ends of heavy lynch ropes, surrounded by a crowd of people laughing. It appeared from the picture that the trees were heavy with grief and the hosts of heaven were in mourning waiting to pour tears from billowing clouds. Now I knew why that picture always brought my father to tears.

A few weeks later, in early 1977, the television networks started promoting a TV mini-series called *Roots*. That was when I started to feel conflict and confusion on my own. In school, we heard very little about black history except in February—Black History Month—and the topic of slavery made me feel exceptionally uncomfortable, like I was being outted. *Roots* traced the history of writer Alex Haley's ancestry back to the original patriarch, Kunta Kinte, and his beautiful life in Africa. The advertisements showed white slave traders attacking a village in Africa, gathering up and dividing his family, and forcing them into slavery in the United States. That's where his name was changed to a slave name: Toby. This ground-breaking historical epic was going to feature just about every black performer from television, stage, and film. My favorite actress at the time was Olivia Cole, a brilliant, soft-spoken performer who starred in after-school specials. She was one of the first African American actresses to cross the color barrier in American TV. She played Kunta Kinte's wife. On the show, they had a daughter together, Kizzi, played by actress Leslie Uggams.

For the first time, I saw beyond what I knew of them as actors. Like black people all over America, I couldn't help seeing the historical members of Alex Haley's family as also my own—the ancestors of all black Americans. *Roots* transformed the lives of all of us. Despite my feelings, however, I was afraid that *Roots* might also be a curse for me. It could easily have ruined my life in Chevy Chase.

Every night for eight nights, my family sat eagerly in the den of our home, fresh popcorn prepared and buttered, lemonade poured over ice, lights dimmed, and waited for *Roots* to begin. My father . . . My mother . . . It seemed that the whole world simply stopped.

As the family sat together, I looked over at my parents.

"It's about time," my mother kept saying, "It's about time."

I called my best friend to share my excitement. "Tina, it's me, are you watching it?"

"Watching what?" she asked.

"*Roots*. Don't tell me you forgot! Turn on channel five, you've only missed the first hour."

"Oh, that movie about the whole slavery thing? Whatever. My parents don't want us to watch it," she said nonchalantly before hanging up the phone on me. Something was happening to us.

That summer I ran into Tina at a concert. She was surrounded by a group of three girls who held themselves at distance from me when I approached, and kept pinching their noses as if they smelled something foul.

"Tina, oh my God! Where have you been? I've called you a million times!"

"I've been busy with orientation stuff at my new school."

"Oh!" I said, wondering if she was going to hug me, as she used to do, or even introduce me to the girls she was with. She chose not to do either.

"Well," she said uncomfortably, "we've got to go, we're meeting some people. See you around."

They turned away from me and met in a giggly huddle, as if I had suddenly become invisible.

"Who was that?" one girl asked in disgust.

"She used to be my best friend," Tina said.

"You were best friends with Kunta Kinte?"

"Not Kunta Kinte," the other girl corrected. "You mean Kizzy." Tina let out a squeal.

"I know," she said, "What was I thinking?"

And just like that, in an echo of laughter and humiliation, while the band onstage played "Freebird," our six-year friendship was over.

❊ ❊ ❊ ❊

My father, Ron Dellums, was a progressive United States Congressman, elected in 1970 from Berkeley, California, to represent California's ninth district. He was a civil and human rights leader and antiwar legislator. In 1971, he drafted and submitted a controversial bill to Congress proposing that the U.S. should cut off all economic support for South Africa, in order to force that country to abandon its policy of Apartheid, the strict segregation of all blacks. I can't imagine what *Roots* must have meant to him.

My mother, Roscoe, though a traditionalist, was an instrumental voice and forceful activist in all of my father's political activities. She was an educator before becoming an attorney, and heavily involved in Africare, an organization providing aid and support to Africa's neediest countries.

In my house, the Pan-African sentiment was on the rise. My father continued to submit his anti-Apartheid legislation to Congress, and it continued to be shot down. I still remember the sorrow that painted his face as he stared out of the living room window, drinking a cup of coffee. Over and over, he repeated something that has always stuck with me: "The time for freedom is always."

It was during this summer that my father explained more to me. He told me that South Africans were separated into three distinctive groups based solely on the color of their skin; Whites, Coloreds (East Indians, Chinese, and those of mixed ethnicities), and Black Africans. It was the Black Africans who had no homes, were forced to separate from their families and mine for gold and diamonds, and had no police protection, human rights, running water, electricity, or medical care, and extremely limited education.

"Piper," he said to me, "it's hard to embrace the lie of freedom when you know that for millions of people it doesn't exist." He sipped from his cup in order to break his will to cry, but the tears ran down anyway. Seeing my father cry changed me.

Soon after, my mother had a visitor from AFS (American Field Service Program), Ms. Paige. They had been friends for years. She had come to ask my mother to consider hosting an international exchange student from Africa for the upcoming school year. With *Roots*, Tina, and the lessons I had learned from my father fresh in my mind, I pleaded and begged for a South African girl to come and live with us. I wanted so desperately to be able to do my part. I wanted to take a child away from the horrors of the slavelike regime and the certain death of mining for precious stones, and give her a family that wasn't divided by governmental brutality, imprisonment, or skin color. But more selfishly, I wanted a friend who shared my face and who could help me find my way out of the woods.

It didn't take long to convince my father, and within a week and a half, we were assigned my African sister, Carrie, from the farmlands of Swaziland.

"What do you think she'll look like?" my brother Erik asked.

"I don't know, but I hope she's a fox!" my other brother, Brandy, added.

I opened up a huge picture book on Africa, one of my mother's many decorative coffee-table books, and found the section on Swaziland. I flipped to a picture of a teen boy with scarification tattoos and sharpened bonelike spears piercing his ears and nose. He was standing next to an elderly woman with a plate in her bottom lip. Her neck had been elongated, like that of a baby giraffe. She had a series of golden rings stacked beneath her chin.

"Oh my God! He's no John Travolta!" I gasped.

"Is that what the girl's going to look like?" Erik asked, his brow furrowed with concern.

"Well, if she does, we won't have to worry about it," Brandy joked. "She'll be hanging out and going to school with Piper."

"Mom, I need you to take me out to get my hair cornrowed and beaded," I demanded, "and the boys and I need some dashikis to wear. I want Carrie to feel at home. I don't want to scare her. If we scare her, she might not want to stay."

By July first, Carrie's arrival date, I had carefully polished and displayed our collection of African art, strategically placed African literature on every table-top, hung a "Welcome" banner written in Zulu, and added a few extra touches that I can now admit might have been overkill.

"Piper!" my mother shouted from the kitchen. "What kind of tribal ceremony are you having upstairs? It sounds like you're calling up a rainstorm for the harvest. We've got plenty of groceries—now turn that music down!"

"But Mom," I called from my bedroom. "I bought this record for Carrie. I'm filling the house with the sounds of the Congo," I said proudly, ignoring the fact that the Congo was nowhere near South Africa.

"No!" my father interjected. "You're calling out the beast in me is what you're doing. Now turn it down before I have to put on my gorilla suit, and for God's sakes, stop burning that incense!" I came down, and moments later, my brothers' friends Danny and Bobby came to the house. Susan Burke, my next-door neighbor and sometimes babysitter, had already arrived. She was Jewish, a well-traveled bohemian, and skilled, at least in her own mind, at applying tribal paint. I thought she did a great job on my face, although my parents probably disagreed. I had written Carrie a poem called "Simunye," which means "We Are One" in Zulu, and wrapped her present in Kinte cloth. I had gotten her what every teenage girl in her right mind would want, the soundtrack of *Saturday Night Fever* and a poster of John Travolta. My mother had picked out a book written by a famous South African writer, called *Cry, the Beloved Country*. We added it to her welcome gifts, but I was certain that she would have already read it.

"They're here, they're here!" echoed through the house. Brandy and Danny came up from the basement. They had been in my dad's gym, shooting pool. We all gathered in the marble foyer around the banner; Dad in his suit, Mom in her Diane von Furstenberg peace-signs mini-dress, Susan in her Janis Joplin hippie outfit, Brandy and Danny in their *Star Trek* convention T-shirts, bell bottoms, and blow-out kit Afros, Erik and Bobby decked out in their usual preppy tennis clothes, and me, face-painted, neck-beaded, hair-braided, in a dashiki and African wrap cloth. Her American family!

The AFS van pulled into our drive. It was filled with teens from all over the world. Some were so amazed at the beauty of the landscaped greenery on our street that they got out to take pictures. Every race seemed represented in that group. It looked as if the teen summit of the United Nations was piling out onto our small suburban street. I can only guess what the neighbors were thinking.

Ms. Paige, my mom's friend, came hurriedly to our front door. She looked pale and nervous, followed by a platinum blonde with big blue eyes and a look of privilege and arrogance that seemed almost too familiar. Before they could reach our front door, Ms. Paige was summoned by the driver back to the van, but the girl continued up our walk and rang the bell.

"Who's that?" I asked my mom.

"Maybe she needs to use our bathroom," my mom said, approaching the door.

"She's a fox!" Brandy added.

"Where's our sister?" I whined, my tribal paint beginning to run.

"Ms. Paige is getting her," my dad said. "Relax, Queen Nefertiti." My mom opened the door. The girl looked at all of us for a moment, then cautiously entered the foyer.

"Will you please inform the congressman and his family that I have arrived?" she said.

"Excuse me . . ." my father started, but before he completed his thought, she pointed to the van.

"You can retrieve my luggage from the boot, and unpack it in my room."

"You packed your clothes in your boot? Either you

have some really small clothes or that's one big boot!"
Erik said. Nobody laughed; we were too uncomfortable. We all just stood there. Erik's friend Bobby
looked around in confusion.

"Where's the African girl?" he said. Just then, Ms.
Paige came bolting through the front door.

"I'm sorry, there seems to be a mistake. Let me
explain," she said. "This is Carrie. The exchange student from Swaziland, South Africa."

"She's Carrie?" I said. "But I thought we request-
ed an authentic African . . . a Black African . . . you
know . . . with black skin!"

"What is going on here?" Carrie asked, standing
defiantly. "I demand to see Congressman Dellums at
once!"

"You're looking at him," my dad stated flatly.

"What is this . . . some kind of American humor?
Well I'll have you know I am not amused," Carrie
snapped, as if we were her property.

"Do you see anyone laughing?" I said. My mother
gave me a harsh look, disappointed at my insensi-
tivity.

The van driver suddenly appeared, holding three
cases of luggage. "We have to go, Ms. Paige," he said.
Ms. Paige was flustered. It was obviously as much of
a shock to her as it was to us.

"I'll call you this evening," she said, "and we can
sort this mess out."

"You're not going to leave me here!" Carrie said, her voice trembling.

We all turned slowly to face her. She burst into tears, her hand tightly held across her mouth.

"God help me!" she gasped, grabbing one of her suitcases and clenching it to her body.

My mother forced a smile and stuttered through the introductions. "These are your American brothers, Brandy and Erik."

"*Qué pasa?*" Brandy said, mimicking his idol, Freddie Prinze from *Chico and the Man*. My mother reached back and pinched him.

"This is your American sister, Piper, and our friends Danny, Bobby, and Susan. You've already met Ron," she stammered, "and I am Roscoe. We're your host parents. You can call us Mom and Dad, if you like." It was the speech she had rehearsed for Carrie when we assumed she was going to be a Black South African, but facing this terrified Afrikanner, it didn't make the warm impression we had hoped for. My father cleared his throat and smiled. "Welcome to your American home."

Carrie turned and ran up the stairs.

"Maybe she really does have to go to the bathroom," Erik said, laughing. We heard a door slam, the familiar click of a lock, and muffled hysteria. Of all fourteen rooms in the house, she had chosen to lock herself in my bedroom. For the next three days.

✶ ✶ ✶ ✶

"I've spoken with Ms. Paige," my mother said. "They're working on getting her a ticket back to South Africa."

"Good," I said smartly. "I'm sick of being in the guest room. I want my room back. She might infest us with her racist germs!"

"Don't be cruel, Piper. You have to understand what a shock this must be for her. She's coming from a country that has engrained fear and prejudice in her. In her country, she probably doesn't associate with any black people outside of her servants. Blacks are considered inferior in her society. Try to remember, she's only a child and she's terrified."

"She's stupid, that's what she is! And if she's touched anything of mine, I'm going tell her just what I think of her!"

"That's enough," my mom said, handing me a tray of food. "Now try to see if she'll open the door to eat anything. The last thing we need is her starving to death in our home." My dad walked in and helped himself to the rest of the food on the stove.

"Wouldn't that make a great headline?" he joked. "White South African Teen Found Dead in Black Congressman's Home."

"It would serve her right," I grumbled. "White South Africans probably starve Black South Africans to death all the time. Let her taste a drop of her own medicine."

"Piper!" my mom said. "We have to approach this child with love. All she knows is the ignorance of anger." I took the tray and rolled my eyes.

"Well, she's about to know my anger in a minute." I knocked on my bedroom door, as I had done every day since she took refuge inside, but as usual, I got no answer. So I made the decision to enter the other way . . . through the bathroom that connected to my room inside and to the hall outside. She jumped when the door opened. I had startled her.

She was sitting on my canopy bed. The poem I had written for her was resting on my pillow. I wondered if she had looked it over more than once.

"My mom made you something to eat," I said. "Eggs, bacon, and toast, but don't count on me serving you all day. You'll have to break yourself of those crazy habits around here." It was clear that she wasn't appreciative of my tone, and I didn't care. I was annoyed with everything about her, her accent, her perfume . . . her face. I offered the food tray to her again, but she chose to continue to ignore me. I don't know what she wanted from me; what she expected, but if she was searching for sympathy, she was out of luck. . . . I had none to spare.

"Well," I said, "I'm just going to leave your breakfast here on my bed, but if you'd like to eat without me staring at you the entire time then you'd better find some words of gratitude for my mother. You see, she's not the hired help."

"Thank you," she snapped. I wouldn't stake my life on it, but I could almost swear that a cold passage of air escaped her lips, sending chills up my spine. She pulled a facecloth from her open suitcase and started wiping off the silverware as if it were crusted with debris.

"What are you afraid of?" I asked her. "Our black rubbing off on the silver?" She dropped the fork onto the tray and started crying, and I felt instantly horrible. My mother was right. I was dealing with the situation all wrong. I took a few deep breaths. With each exhalation I released some of my anger until I was able to find some remnant of compassion within myself. I sat on the bed beside her and rubbed her back gently. I thought she might flinch or move away from me, but she didn't.

"I'm sorry," I said. "I was being really nasty. I didn't mean to make you cry." She shook her head and lifted her eyes to meet mine. She looked different this time. The tears had made something almost beautiful appear in her stare. We looked at each other for what felt like an eternity. I saw her as if for the first time . . . the frightened young teen uprooted from a world of lies and homes surrounded by electric barbed wire in order to give the illusion of safety. And I believe that she saw me, and though it contradicted everything she had been taught, she saw *me*. I opened my arms, not knowing what would happen next. But it worked, and she leaned in to hug me back. It was definitely an uncomfortable hug, but it was real.

"I'm sorry, too," she whispered.

"I'll forgive you if you let me move you into the guest room," I said jokingly. "I've had to wear this tribal dress all weekend!" I helped her repack her things and carried her suitcases down the hall.

"Did you like the poem I wrote you? 'Simunye' is a Zulu word. It means 'We are one.'"

"Yeah, I know what it means. Zulu is one of the most popular of the ten languages spoken in my country. I loved the poem. Thank you."

"Did you open your presents?"

"Of course I did. Everyone at home is going to be quite jealous. You can't purchase records and books like these where I come from."

"That doesn't make any sense. My mother said *Cry, the Beloved Country* was written by a South African."

"Maybe," she said. "I wouldn't know. Certain kinds of literature are banned in my country. It's the only way to protect us."

"Protect you from what?"

"I don't know. That's just the way it is." I didn't understand what she was saying. How is it possible for a government to decide what you can and cannot read or see? It sounded a bit like the white South Africans were also enslaved . . . but they were oblivious to it.

"Are you allowed to go to the cinema here?" she asked me.

"Well sure, we have movie theaters all over the place. Is there a particular film you'd like to see?" The pause that followed made it clear that we were not talking about the same thing. I thought I knew what she had asked me, "Am I allowed to go to the cinema?" Then it clicked. She literally wanted to know whether I, as a black person, had the legal right to watch a movie inside of a theater.

"Well of course I am!"

"Of course you are what?" she asked, as if she had no idea of what I was responding to.

"Allowed to go to the movies. Isn't that what you wanted to know?"

"What does your passbook say that you are?" she asked.

"What's a passbook?"

"You know." She continued, "It's probably called something different in your language. I'm speaking of the identification card that gives your racial category and states your mobility boundaries and curfew hours." She was sounding stranger to me by the minute.

"We don't have anything like that here."

"How do the police and government keep tabs on the day-to-day whereabouts of the blacks in this country?"

"Why would the police and government need to keep tabs on black people?"

"It's not safe for them to be just wandering in the streets."

"Not safe? What are you talking about?"

"Well, in my country, many of the blacks try to stir up trouble and mess things up for the obedient blacks, so this way, the government can separate the agitators from everyone else."

"That's crazy. Are you telling me that all Black South Africans have to carry around identification books in their own country?"

"It's not their country. It's our country. Some blacks have 'honorary white' status, if they're important blacks, like your father. But the majority would be totally lost without government intervention." I felt sick to my stomach. Even more so because of her look of absolute innocence.

"No, Carrie," I said, "they wouldn't be lost. They'd be free."

* * * *

The first month took some adjusting for all of us.

Carrie was used to having all of her needs and wants met by servants—from what and when she wanted to eat, to where and when she wanted to be driven—so we had to clench our teeth through many of her demands and expectations of us. At first, it truly seemed to confuse her that we were not paralyzed by our own independent thought and actions, though she soon learned she was going to be treated as an equal member of our family.

"Good morning, Piper," she said the next morning, having entered my room without knocking. "I've left my dirty towels and linens by the door to be washed. Could you please fetch me some clean towels, and draw me a bath? It's such a beautiful morning, I thought I'd take a walk."

"Do you have arthritic hands?" I asked her, flipping over my pillow. She examined her fingers for a moment. "Arthritic hands at my age?" She laughed. "I'm only sixteen."

"Do you have palsy or any other crippling disease I should know about?"

"No. I'm perfectly healthy."

"Well, good," I said. "Then there's no reason why you can't knock before entering, drop your own clothes in the laundry chute, get anything you need out of the linen closet, and draw your own bath. Right?"

It took a second for her to understand what I was getting at, but she did.

"Right," she said, backing out of my room.

That Saturday morning marked the birth of our

establishing a civil relationship with one another, and set the stage for what would soon become mutual respect and trust.

I was surprised to find out that in Africa she had never seen lions, monkeys, or giraffes, except at the zoo, and that she didn't know how to swim because the oceans were quite a distance from her home. She seemed even less African then she looked. In my mother's coffee-table books there were incredible pictures of the African people living in harmony with the great beasts of the wild, and yet Carrie hadn't experienced anything substantially more exotic than the average teen in the States had.

"I thought you'd be more like Tarzan and less like normal people," I said, realizing how ridiculous that sounded after the words had already left my lips.

"Not all of Africa is a jungle." She laughed. "I live in a place that's not as sophisticated or built up as yours, but we have all the civilized comforts of the rest of the world. We don't hunt for leopard skins, ivory tusks, zebra, and other large game. We don't ride on elephants' backs or wrestle crocodiles. That would be barbaric. We have herds of farm animals. You know, sheep, goats, and cows. But I'll tell you one significant difference. We kill our fowl and meat fresh before eating it; we rarely purchase it frozen and packaged like you do."

The idea kind of made me sick, and seemed as if it

would be incredibly messy and time-consuming. I was more grateful than ever for our local grocery store.

"It must take a lot of time preparing dinner," I said.

"I don't know. We have Mary and Rutha to take care of meals for us."

I knew that she was speaking of her black servants although she seemed to believe that they were her "friends." I wonder how long the friendship would last if Mary and Rutha had the freedom to choose their own destiny?

"They must be worn out at the end of each day," I said, feeling a pain in my heart for the two women who probably worked seven days a week, twenty hours a day, for the equivalent of fifteen dollars a month.

"Oh no, they enjoy cleaning house and laundering linen, but I'm sure they love killing the animals to prepare our meals most of all; it's natural for them. And anyway, they get to keep whatever parts of the animal we don't need." I couldn't believe what I was hearing. This was more bizarre than *The Twilight Zone*.

"Lucky them!" I said sarcastically. I knew I had to get away. "Well, Carrie, I've got some little errands to run. I am going to go get a bus." I tried to get out of the room as quickly as I could, but then, "Give me a chance to freshen up and I'll go with you. How exciting, a bus and everything!" she said before dashing for the bathroom . . . the same bathroom I was headed for. I lifted my head toward the heavens. Help!

Carrie had never been on a public bus before, and I could tell she was a little uncomfortable being so closely surrounded by unfamiliar people, and yet, there was a hint of excitement that her face couldn't hide. I pointed out our school and where the bus would let us off and pick us up each day.

"The school is huge!" she said, keeping her eyes on it, until it was no longer in view.

"Don't worry about it, you'll find your way around all right," I said.

We spent a great deal of time window-shopping that day, and pointing out things that we would one day own. She had exquisite taste in art and a great laugh that made the afternoon more than bearable. I took her to the best hamburger place in Chevy Chase. Sitting at our table, we both opened our mouths to speak and said the exact same thing: "John Travolta!" A movie poster for John Travolta in *Grease* beckoned from across the street. That was the most profound transition in our relationship. Through our shared love for John Travolta, we were about to become great friends. We paid the bill quickly, grabbed hands (for the very first time), and ran laughing to the movie theater. We sat through *Grease* three consecutive times, hiding under the seats between shows to avoid buying new tickets.

✳ ✳ ✳ ✳

My mother also began spending a great deal of time with Carrie. She took her to social gatherings, to see African American prima ballerina Sandra Butler perform for the Capital Ballet Company, to the Smithsonian, to the home of Frederick Douglass, back and forth to Capitol Hill to watch my father in action on the floor of Congress and at press conferences, and to a reception in honor of his peace talks in Cuba.

"Your father is such an important and respected leader in this country," Carrie said to me one night while swinging on the hammock in our backyard. We were watching for shooting stars. "He is always surrounded by crowds and cameras. There are so many people that seem eager just to shake his hand and listen to him speak. I've never seen so many different types of people come to see one man. In my country we have white leaders for the white people, and tribal chiefs who are honored only by members of their own respective group."

"Don't the people get to vote for whomever they want to lead the nation?" I asked.

"The white people are the only ones who are allowed to vote. Black Africans will never vote in South Africa," she said, her voice cracking with remorse. She was changing, blossoming. She was feeling compassion and recognizing her own anger about the things she'd been taught to believe. She was becoming an American teenager.

I wanted her mind to stay elevated and hopeful.

"My dad says to never say never because then you kill your dreams."

She kissed my forehead.

"Then let us dream together," she whispered.

✶ ✶ ✶ ✶

Soon my father went away again. The brutal beating death of South African activist Steven Biko while being held in a South African jail incited international demands for justice. Amnesty International and other human rights organizations were drawing public awareness toward the practices of the Apartheid regime, and Carrie was torn between her loyalties to our family and the lies she had been fed by her family back home. We had a few tiffs and disagreements, the kind that sisters are supposed to have, but tensions ran higher than expected after the devastating incident that happened to Erik in late February. No matter how hard we tried to escape it, the universe continued to paint our world in black and white.

You would have thought that the prettiest girl in school had said "yes" to our entire family on the day of my brother Erik's first "big date." My mother was clearly the most excited, taking pictures of his every move and welling up with tears each time she thought about how quickly her baby was growing up. Carrie and I helped pick out his clothes, and Brandy gave him private pointers on how to know the perfect time to steal the first kiss. I'll never forget how handsome he looked, roses in one hand, box of chocolates in the other, making his way down our steep hill to the bus stop. Carrie couldn't get over how freely whites and blacks dated and married in the U.S.

Erik couldn't have been gone for more than thirty minutes or so when Carrie heard him crying on the porch outside. He was drenched from head to toe in bright white house paint. He never made it to the date, never even got on the bus, because a group of older teens had decided that they wanted to teach him a lesson about being black.

"My God! Erik, what happened to you?" she gasped.

"The first time they drove past they asked me if I was lost, and then yelled some racial crap out the window and took off. I don't know . . . I didn't think they were going to come back."

Carrie woke me up in the middle of that very same night. Her mind was troubled, and she was having a hard time sleeping.

"I think some things are worse in your country than they are in mine," she said. "In my country we may have a crazy system of government, but at least it is clear to everyone what is accepted and what will not be tolerated. It's all very clear. But in this country you never know what you're up against. Here, you believe that you have all the answers, and yet even the congressman's son is seen only as a black boy when he's spotted at the bus stop alone."

✶ ✶ ✶ ✶

The end of school marked the final weeks of Carrie's stay with us in the U.S. No one was prepared to say good-bye, and we were all very careful not to bring up the subject. I think we secretly hoped that by ignoring it, we could avoid it. Carrie and I both knew that I would never be welcomed in her home, and that what we had shared together was only going to continue in memory, but we talked about planning a visit just to ease the pain of knowing it would never happen.

AFS hosted a farewell dance for all of the students who had participated in the program. Some chose to make public speeches about how valuable their experiences in the States had been. Carrie was one of those students, and she spoke eloquently about how her life had so dramatically changed.

"I am leaving with the tools necessary to fight injustice and mend the bridges of broken humanity all over the world," she said. "*Simunye!* We are one people, one nation, one family!"

We spent our last night together in the forest across the street from my house. We made promises to write and to one day see each other again, but when she climbed onto the bus the next morning, I knew that I was seeing her for the last time. She wrote many letters to me and to my family, telling us all about the progressive student political movement she was involved with, working actively to abolish the

Apartheid system. She was sharing banned literature and her experiences in America hoping to expose the truth in a nation that killed their own people to hide it. She took a very dangerous and unpopular stand . . . and stuck to it to the end. For a time we kept closely in contact with her. She sounded happy and strong.

But then very suddenly her letters just stopped. In her letters, she had written about her fear and how dangerous it was becoming there. Some of her political friends had disappeared. Soon our letters started coming back stamped "Return to Sender" in Afrikaans. I collected articles and pictures to send, but now I had no place to send them.

I missed her. I missed my friend, her laughter, her smile; she was the sister I never had, and she was suddenly gone.

* * * *

We spent years searching for her, even enlisting the embassy's help, but our search kept coming up with nothing. It was as if she had never existed. Somehow, Carrie had simply vanished. Thousands of South African political activists were sent away or exiled during that time period, and thousands more killed or assumed dead.

My father continued to offer "The Dellums Bill," against South African Apartheid to Congress for the next fifteen long years. Finally, in 1986, H.R. 1580, the Anti-Apartheid Act, was passed imposing economic sanctions on South Africa. In 1991 Apartheid was abolished, and in 1994 former political prisoner Nelson Mandela became the first black man elected president in South Africa.

It's funny how the mind works. Every time I see John Travolta, I think of Carrie. Something magical happened to both of us in 1977, we found our way out of the woods and into each other's hearts. Nineteen-seventy-seven was our time, but what my father said was right: "The time for freedom is always." I know that even if she was killed and her body returned to the earth, the time we shared will live on in my heart forever.

piper dellums

Following the events of "Simunye," **PIPER DELLUMS** studied South African politics and South African literature at the University of California at Berkeley, where she became an anti-Apartheid activist. She later became an active member of Amnesty International, Hollywood Women's Political Committee, Equality Now, and Artists for a Free South Africa.

Later, Dellums moved her family to Johannesburg, South Africa, where she "aided in building some of the first black homes post-Apartheid and experienced years of turmoil, unrest, fear, and magnificent beauty." She describes Black South Africans as "tender, spiritual, humble, and intelligent people with awesome capacity for forgiveness."

Dellums's time with Carrie, her Afrikaaner soul mate, strongly influenced her life. "Experiences such as these are not the sort that get stored away in the back files of one's memories," she states. "They are the precious, life-altering sort that silently guide and alter the paths of one's journeys through life."

In 2000, the Disney Channel adapted the story of Carrie into an Emmy and NAACP Image Award–winning film, *The Color of Friendship*. Dellums notes,

"The film has touched the lives of millions of families with its bold expose of racism and tolerance."

Dellums currently lives back in Northern California, where she teaches for a private Jewish high school and teaches, directs, and produces children's theater in other schools. She has two daughters, Sydney Lauren, ten, and Dylan Jade, eight. "Oh . . . and before I forget," she writes, "John Travolta is still amazing!!"

Mayah in 1976, only five years old and already so serious about la maternelle *(nursery school).*

little american mom, big french briefcase

(or, what i think my daughter would have to say about her mother)

by SUSIE MORGENSTERN

AFTER MY PARENT'S wedding, Papa had given it a try in exotic New Jersey but he couldn't take it in the U.S. They didn't speak French, they didn't eat French, and they didn't even like the French, something that was totally reciprocal as far as he was concerned. So Mom decided she would be the flexible one and move to France. Big deal, what difference did it make when you were in loooove. She would tell people, "It could be worse. . . . Albania or something."

She knew a total of three words when she arrived in France: "hello," which was *bonjour*, "thank you," which was *merci,* and what she thought was "good-bye": *allez-vous en.* She thought people were rude when they reacted strongly to this expression. Little did she suspect that her mistaken version of "good-bye" meant "go away!" or "hit the road." But this was far from being her only problem.

Okay, the language was mystery number one, the money that she had to keep converting into dollars was mystery number two, the weights and measures in kilos and grams were mystery number three, and I think her magical mystery list went way into the hundreds. But I never saw anything particularly dramatic, as she was just my mother and the look of incomprehension that glazed her eyes dozens of times a day seemed quite normal to me. She would wrinkle up her face, thinking that what she was missing in the fast-flowing French that people were spitting by her was of the utmost importance, when actually it was some banal remark about the weather or how cute I was.

The first time I realized there was a problem with my mother was the first day of nursery school, ironically called *la maternelle,* which also means "motherly." I was really excited. It was, after all, my big day. But my mom looked like she had swallowed sixty frog's legs and eighty-five snails. She was green and gray and gruesome. When we arrived at the gate of the school, I tried to give her back her hand, but she tightened her grip and I feared she would never let me go. There were kids screaming and crying as if they were going to the slaughterhouse but I wasn't one bit scared. I just wanted my hand back. One by one these other three-year-olds were given a gentle push through the gate, where apparently kindly teachers were waiting. Only my mother stood there watching and seething. Fathers were saying *"Travaille bien!"* (Work hard!) to their sons in short pants that covered their baby fat, as they abandoned them on the threshold of real life. Mothers had those same words to offer their child laborers. Work hard! Work well. Work!

My mother had this scowl and stared at me with her eternal question in English: "What am I doing here?" Sometimes she'd add: "Get me out of here!" That morning she went on to say: "Why are they telling these little babies to work hard? What are they going to make you do in there? You're only three years old! How can I leave you in this work camp?"

When finally we were the last ill-assorted little couple standing there as if we had missed the train, the principal came out and said *"Madame . . ."* My mother hugged me and held on to me for dear life as if she would never see me again in this incomprehensible world of woe, and she proclaimed most emphat-

ically for all to hear, *"Have fun!"* clinging to the clos-
ing gate with tiny tears dripping down her chubby
cheeks. She was still standing there at the end of the
day with her arms wide open and a smile that went
from the far west to the extreme east. I don't remember what we did that first day in nursery school, but I
think we probably did work hard *and* have fun doing
it, and so I obeyed both the French parents and my
own American mother, so American she could have
been draped in stars and stripes.

Even before *la maternelle*, Mom had sold me down
the river and stowed me away in *la crêche*, a French day
care center. She said she felt guilty every minute of her
life from the second she abandoned me wrinkled and
unkempt in the morning to the second she picked me up
all starched and clean, ironed, perfumed, and coiffed.

When I finished *la maternelle* and had to go to
real school, first grade, she did not buy me a backpack or a book bag, which were not only *not* in fashion in France but not available. Instead she had to
purchase one of the enormous briefcases all the
French schoolchildren wore strapped to their backs.
If this wasn't enough to give her a nervous break-
down, there was the list of school supplies to deal
with. The death sentence had already been banned in
France, but we feared some other dramatic punish-
ment if we were not equipped with the items on the
official list. She had to spend days among the hordes

of other parents on this treasure hunt to find just the right sized paper with the precise number of millimetered lines, and just the exact brand of pencils and rulers and pens and ink and dozens of items nobody in the world carried. She was indignant and outraged. Out loud.

Then when all these bizarre objects took their place in my briefcase, along with the manuals and notebooks (not supplied by the public school), she strapped it to her own back and bent over in two, prophesying that I'd break my spinal column if I carried it myself. There was no way she would let me be my own beast of burden and ruin my back for life. She insisted on carrying it all the time and then she'd hand it to me in front of everyone in a gesture that tried to make a political statement.

We had school Monday, Tuesday, Thursday, Friday, and Saturday morning. These Saturday mornings were really the last straw, but there were a lot of last straws. There was a lot of homework, and she considered homework an encroachment on her quality time with me.

I'd rush home at her side as she crumbled under the weight of my briefcase. "What's the hurry?" she'd say.

"Oh my God, Mom, I have so much homework to do!"

"Just don't do it!" she'd repeat each day.

"That's easy to say!" I'd spit with wrath. "Think

how happy you'd be if I stayed back, if I never went to college, if I ended up being the last in the class!"

Every day she would write a letter full of French mistakes: "Mayah couldn't do her homework today because she had a headache." (This she would replace with sore throats, blisters on the fingers, rashes, canker sores, pest, and cholera, or anything else that came to her mind. One of her favorites was pure wishful thinking: visiting relatives from the U.S.) "Please excuse her." She never learned to write the long French formula to sign off a letter. It sounded silly and pompous to her American ears: "Please accept the expression of my distinguished sentiments." Instead she'd sign it "Love, Madame Morgenstern," which was equally hypocritical because she certainly did not love my teacher. I accepted the letter she handed me *and put it in my desk drawer* every single day of my school life just to avoid an antihomework pep talk, and then despite her, I'd sit down obediently, apply myself to the assignments, and organize my briefcase for the next day. When I was finished it would be dinnertime and then bedtime. The French have an expression for their working lives "*Métro, boulot, dodo*" ("subway, work, sleep"). Mom would say "School, homework, school." She'd also holler to me, "Lincoln freed the slaves!" I had no idea who this Lincoln was, but I got the gist of it.

She'd go to every parent-teacher conference so as to further scratch the infected mosquito bite. Every parent there was convinced that better education meant *more* homework, whereas she would single-handedly fight against this sadistic practice, maintaining that it was unhealthy and illegal.

One man said to her: "You, the assassin of the Redskins, you have the nerve to come and tell us how to educate our children in France!"

I would cringe and die whenever she risked speaking French in public. She had such a thick accent you could hardly tell she was speaking French at all. She never actually studied French, she just picked it up (or didn't!). And as soon as she'd pick me up at school, she'd try to switch off my French side. "Speak English!" she'd order. If I reverted to French, she'd play deaf and walk ahead of me. So I'd run to tell my father all the latest gossip and little tales of school news. It was just so much easier for me in French. The same went for my older sister.

Mom would look crushed and insulted at our defection to Papa. She'd say something to him in English through the wall of the kitchen and he'd inevitably respond in French with a *"Quoi?"* (What?). To which she would in turn grunt, "What did you say?" To which Papa would admit (in French) to having said nothing. This linguistic ping-pong became silence during our meals. They couldn't decide which language to speak, which of them would be cowardly enough to cede their identity and national heritage, so they kept ruthlessly, brutally quiet.

The only time Mom authorized me to use French was when she begged me to speak for her. "Ask the grocery man for a kilo of onions." "Describe the symptoms to the doctor." "Tell the clerk my administrative problems." These were the times she thought it better they not identify her as a foreigner for fear of inferior and hostile treatment. In a way, I liked my role of being a mother to my mother. She needed me, and that gave me an unusual power children rarely have.

Even when other parents stopped coming for their kids after school, Mom was stubbornly, steadfastly there. I could have walked home with my sister, or alone. After all, I was going on eleven and resented having this overwhelming mother as omnipresent as when I was in nursery school. My teacher, Monsieur Ginesi, was an environmentalist. When he went on and on about the dangers of the sun in our Riviera town of Nice and how we should avoid sunbathing, *voilà!* There would be my mother flaunting her dark brown tan all year round. Monsieur Ginesi was not a fan of imperialistic Americans with their fizzy soda and silly hamburgers, while Mom waited for me sip-ping from the can of Diet Coke eternally perched in her right hand. Monsieur Ginesi said he thought Americans were poorly dressed, while my mother would model her torn jeans and a man's big shirt. Monsieur Ginesi thought Americans were loud and indiscrete. My mother would comply by bursting out with a shrill *Mayah* as soon as I came into view. I'd run and try to reach her before she could do any more damage. I always felt that these displays of excitement should have been saved for more important things.

If she had to send a note to the teacher, I would write it and she would sign it. Sometimes she tried to do my homework. She'd write what she thought was a brilliant composition and be furious when she only got 7 out of 20. "I have a bloody Ph.D. and I can't pass fifth grade." She was sure that she would never have gotten out of high school in France. Her Ph.D. in comparative literature was being studied by a team of linguists in the University of Aix-en-Provence to understand the mistakes Anglo-Saxons make in French. What Mom considered important clashed dramatically with the philosophy of 99 percent of my teachers. Her criteria were originality, spark, thrust, fantasy, and humor. I guess humor was the worst of her offenses. I myself couldn't stand it every time she would try to make light of the worst of my human tragedies (like getting a 7 out of 20 in composition). If I cried because of a bad mark, she'd say, "What's the matter? Your mother died?"

She seemed a contented enough person. She was always busy and bustling and bursting with joy and pride in my good marks and in certain things I would say. The shadow in her life was missing her own mother and sisters across the sea at a time when phoning was too expensive for convivial conversation and reserved only for birth, death, illness, and other crises. She'd plan our summer trips to the U.S. all year, and that would appease her longing. She was peaceful and quite happy with my father and us. She was certainly getting used to France. Her only bone of contention remained school. This got worse, not better, as we advanced.

In sixth grade I started to study English, which, of course, I already spoke. I could have taken German like the smart kids did. German separates the men from the boys. English is for the dunces. I would have liked to be in the elite, but Mom insisted that I learn to read and write English and then proceeded to regret her decision especially when I'd go over the grammar exercises with her, pronouncing everything in the stuffy fake British accent of my French English teacher. The idea of "native" teachers hadn't been born. My mother thought my teacher spoke English like her own Ukranian grandmother! When I really wanted to drive Mom crazy, I'd exit from the kitchen dramatically like a Shakespearean actress, saying "I think I'll have a baahth!"

Sometimes, rarely, she'd cooperate with the system, like when I woke up in the black of night in a panic and said, "Ma, Ma, I'm late for school!" She jumped up, ran down the stairs, started the car and drove me to school in her nightgown. "Funny there's not a car on the road!" she said shivering with nothing on her bare arms. When she saw the school gate was locked and not a soul around, she realized something was wrong. That's when I looked at my watch to see that it was only four in the morning.

Whatever the tragic occasion or the dramatic situation, she had this excessive exuberance and overeager optimism. How I hated her daily refrain: "Don't worry about it! It's nothing! It'll be okay." Okay? Pure American philosophy! Tests? Academic competitions? Report cards? Don't worry? She'd say it but she didn't do it. I suspect that she herself stopped breathing when I took a test. And then she'd meet me out of breath at the door and say, "Soooooooooo? How did it go?" And when I'd report catastrophe, failure, traps, and mental blocks, she would laugh it off with "It doesn't matter" and "Just don't worry!" And I wanted to strangle her.

And despite having a Ph.D., she was completely lost in the French system. She was administratively illiterate, couldn't fill out the medical forms, couldn't write a check. And so when it was time for my sister to take the baccalaureate exams (ridiculously hard exams required to get out of high school), Mom gave up sleeping and eating—except eating herself up—and lived to devote herself entirely to her favorite sport: worrying. She said that the week her daughter took the "bac" was the week she grew old.

To us she bluffed and lied and claimed she wasn't one bit worried. She was absolutely convinced we were superior. She just didn't want an impartial outsider to challenge that conviction.

Well, we both eventually made it and mom was so relieved I actually overheard her telling someone that she was making peace with her old enemy the Ministère de l'Education Nationale, French Ministry of Education.

We'd notice from summer to summer in the U.S.A. that Mom wasn't as blatantly American as her sisters. She wasn't American, she wasn't exactly French, she was something else, some kind of mutant with half a foot in each world. That's why she always looked like she was limping.

"Life isn't that simple," she'd tell me when I said I hated something I had liked the day before. I was often ashamed of her in public, and yet I was secretly proud of being a little bit different.

Thanks to her I had not one but two cultures, two languages, two worlds. I was thankful to have only one mother. But I never told her that. Life isn't that simple.

susie morgenstern

Born in Newark, New Jersey, **SUSIE MORGENSTERN** earned a B.S. from Rutgers University and the University of Jerusalem. She received an M.A. and doctorate in comparative literature from the University of Nice, where she has now been a professor for thirty-two years. She began writing in French shortly after her marriage to a French mathematician who—along with her two daughters—helped correct her work.

An immensely popular children's book author in France, she has won too many prizes and awards there to count. Among her American accolades are two Mildred L. Batchelder honors for *Secret Letters from 0 to 10* (1999) and *A Book of Coupons* (2001). Known for expertly adopting the point of view of children and adolescents and incorporating day-to-day life in her books, Morgenstern believes she touches young readers because "words that come from the heart enter the heart."

Other books published in the United States include: *Three Days Off* (2001), *Princesses Are People, Too: Two Modern Fairy Tales* (2002), and a forthcoming middle-grade novel called *Sixth Grade*. She tries to visit the United States frequently, but her daughters and grandchildren now happily occupy her time in France. Writing the story about her relationship with French schools made her realize how nostalgic she is about the wonderful period in which her children were growing up in a strange culture. She tells all young parents, "Enjoy every minute! It flies by so fast."

Here we are, the crew of Godfathers Inc. *outside our barracks in the fall of 1944, just before we went overseas. From left to right there's Joe Heustess, our engineer; Mike Brennan, our radio operator; Bill O'Malley, our ball-turret gunner; me, Harry Mazer, the waist gunner; Byron Young, our tailgunner; and Harry Grey, nose gunner and togglier.*

join the army and see the world

By HARRY MAZER

WHEN I TURNED seventeen, the world was in the midst of World War II. I volunteered for the Army Air Cadets, dreaming that I would become a pilot and fly across continents. The following year—it was July 1943, and I had just graduated from high school—I waited at Penn Station for a train that would take me to an undisclosed army base, where I would begin my training. My parents were with me, and my kid brother. As I boarded the train and waved good-bye, my mother regarded me sorrowfully.

"Don't worry, Mom," I said. "I'll be okay."

I was glad to be off. I made a friend right away. He was a worried sort of guy. "Where do you think they're taking us?" he said.

I threw my hands up. "Wherever!" I didn't know and I didn't care. Away from home for the first time in my life, I was interested in everything. I had pored over atlases and maps, read names I couldn't pronounce. Now I was actually going to those places. Nothing bothered me, not the stifling heat, not the open coach cars, not the cinders I kept picking out of my eyes; not even having to sleep sitting up all the way to Miami Beach.

A month of basic training in Miami Beach. Then Grove City, Pennsylvania, for five months of college, including ten hours of flight training in Piper Cubs. And finally to San Antonio, Texas, for classification. Would I be a pilot, navigator, or bombardier?

"Pilot," I said to my buddies.

"Keep your fingers crossed."

The tests went on for two days, but when the names were posted mine wasn't on any of the officer lists.

"Washed out," I said. The man next to me was crying. He didn't see his name, either.

I didn't cry, but it was hard to take.

I was shipped off to Dyersburg, Tennessee, where I volunteered for gunnery school. Almost overnight it seemed, I was a gunner on a B-17, the Flying Fortress, the big four-engine bomber of that war.

My crew was assembled and did its final training in Alexandria, Louisiana. There were ten of us on the plane, three officers and seven enlisted men, and every man except the pilots was responsible for a gun. Our pilot was twenty-one and wore his officer's cap cocked over one eye. The co-pilot, at twenty-seven, was the old man on the crew. His wife had just had a baby, and we declared ourselves the baby's godfathers; then, since every crew named its own plane, we called ours *Godfathers, Inc.*

My best friend on the crew was Mike Brennan, a tall, skinny redhead. He and I were both eighteen years old. We were the boys from the Bronx, the only New Yorkers on the crew. We had grown up only a few miles apart. He was first generation Irish Catholic, and I was first generation Polish Jewish.

Our girlfriends were both from the Bronx, and Mike kept saying that when the war ended the four of us were going to double-date.

"What are we going to do, Brennan?"

"I don't know, Mazer. Go to a nightclub."

"You ever been in a nightclub, Brennan?"

"Have you, Mazer?"

"Just as much as you, Brennan."

"They're not going to let you in, Mazer."

"How are they going to keep me out, Brennan, when I'm in uniform and I've got all these medals?"

"What medals, Mazer? You don't even have a good conduct medal, yet."

"Brennan, I'm working on it."

✦ ✦ ✦ ✦

We flew overseas in a brand new B-17G Flying Fortress. It was a long flight from Lincoln, Nebraska, to Bangor, Maine, then over to Goose Bay, Labrador, where ice and below-zero weather grounded us for two weeks. It was right after Christmas 1944 that we crossed the Atlantic, passing by Greenland, refueling in Reykjavik, Iceland, and landing finally at an airfield near Royston, a tiny English village just north of London. A Bronx boy who had never left home before, I had become a world traveler.

Over the next months, February, March, and April 1945, our crew flew twenty-five bombing missions, most over Germany, often through heavy enemy fire. On every mission there were losses, planes hit, engines knocked out, men wounded. Harry Gray, our nose gunner, was wounded, and Mike and I went to see him in the hospital.

"You're lucky," I said. "You got the million-dollar wound." He'd taken a piece of flak in the meaty part of his butt. "If I'm gonna get hit, that's the place."

"Too close to home," Mike said.

"Where do you want it?"

"I don't want it anyplace."

"I know, but if you had your choice?"

Mike held up his little finger. "The tip," he said. "Can I go home now?"

We were all nervous. It was April 1945, and the war was so close to being over. Our armies were in Germany, and there weren't a lot of big bombing targets left. We hadn't flown in nearly two weeks. Maybe we wouldn't have to fly again.

Then, on April 24, we got word that we were going to fly a mission the next day. That night, I woke up and I couldn't get back to sleep. Mice raced along the shelf near my head, threatening my cache of Lorna Doone cookies and Lucky Strike cigarettes. I heard the ping of the hot stove, and in its glow I saw Mike asleep in the bunk below me.

In the morning, Mike and I walked through the darkness to the briefing room. It was still early, and we sat in back, drinking coffee and talking. When the briefing officer appeared, the room got quiet. He pulled back the curtain to show a map of Europe.

"Our target is Plzen, Czechoslovakia," he said.

Plzen was home of Skoda, a major munitions factory, heavily defended by German anti-aircraft guns.

Standing in the back of a truck as we rode out to our plane, I felt the weight of the .45 revolver strapped under my jacket. Guns had been issued to us after reports of captured American airmen being killed and strung up on telephone poles along the main highways.

At the plane, we loaded guns and ammunition and checked fuel levels. I stood by as, one after another, the engines were started. The last thing I did was scoot under the plane and pull out the heavy chocks holding the wheels.

For takeoff, the tail gunner, Byron Young, the ball turret gunner, Bill O'Malley, and I squeezed into Mike's radio compartment in the rear of the plane. The four of us sat with our knees up, backs against the bomb bay partition. Takeoff was always tense. The heavily loaded planes mostly got off the ground, but sometimes they didn't and men and planes were blown up.

We'd been kidding around, but when our turn came to take off and the roar of the engines filled the plane, I pressed my back against the wall, listening, waiting, urging the plane up. The plane lumbered slowly down the runway.

"Go!" Mike yelled. We were all yelling at the pilot, the plane. "Move this shit-kicker."

Once we were in the air, we cheered. "Everybody breathe now," Mike said.

We went back to our positions. I hooked up the intercom and checked my oxygen line. I wore my parachute harness, the chute beside me on the floor ready to hook in place if needed. Mike and I had talked a lot about what we'd do if we had to jump. We'd never practiced. More than once he'd said, "Would you have the nerve?"

"If I had to." I shrugged. I didn't know.

It was still dark and I had to watch for other planes that might accidentally swing too close. When we finally broke through the clouds and into the light, the sky was full of planes, big four-engine bombers everywhere, bobbing and rising into position like ships at sea.

At 10,000 feet, I put on my oxygen mask. Once we were over Germany, I was on the watch for enemy fighters. We were at 26,000 feet when we reached our bombing altitude. It was a perfect spring day, with only a few clouds in the sky. The gray smudgy flak that marked the bursting anti-aircraft shells had begun to stain the sky.

Flak was a constant, steel fragments that burst through the planes like birdshot through a tin can. At the end of each mission, we counted the holes. I wore a steel helmet, goggles, and a bullet-proof vest, and crouched on every extra bullet-proof vest I could find. That extra protection had saved me more than once.

"Flak at six o clock." Young, the tail gunner, said. His voice was tight over the intercom.

The flak grew more intense as we entered the bomb run. It was all around us. At the last moment, clouds obscured the target, and our squadron circled for another try. It was on that second run that we were hit.

The plane shuddered, tilted, and I went down. Ammo box and flak suits landed on top of me. My intercom and oxygen lines were torn loose. I crawled to the port window. The wing was blown away, both engines gone. Only a stump remained.

I looked down the tunnel to the tail position. Young was gone. O'Malley had climbed up out of the ball turret and was snapping his chute in place. I was at the door. Red emergency hinges. I pulled the releases, then pushed the door. Pushed . . . pushed . . . I couldn't get it open.

I turned my back to the door. O'Malley was behind me. Mike stood in the doorway of the radio compartment. I was dizzy. No oxygen. No air. *Mike! Come on!* I threw myself against the door and fell out of the plane.

My foot caught in the door, and I hung outside the plane, the tail assembly looming above me. I hung there for a moment, and then I fell away.

I didn't pull my chute. There was no calculation, no thought. The drill was *Count to ten and then pull the handle.* A chute can easily get tangled in a falling plane. I fell. I didn't pull my chute. I was falling, but it didn't feel like falling. It was like being on a mattress, except for the pressure and pain in my ears and the goggles that had come loose and were battering me in the face.

I don't know how long or how far I fell. We were five miles up when our plane was hit.

I was on my back and I couldn't see where I was going, and I didn't know how to turn myself over. I fell. I was above the clouds, aware of them below me, and then I was in them.

I don't remember pulling the handle on my chute. It burst open and hit me in the face like a basket of wet laundry. I blacked out. When I came to I was dangling from my parachute.

I remember the sky, that calm, untroubled blue sky, bluer and emptier than any sky I'd ever known. Our plane had vanished. The six hundred planes on the mission—all gone. In the distance, a thick column of black smoke rose from the ground. Nearer, but too far to be sure, I saw two other parachutes. I thought the one below me was Young and the one above me O'Malley. I searched the sky for Mike, but there were no other parachutes.

I was descending slowly, too slowly. I felt exposed, vulnerable, a wide-open target for anyone with a gun. Then, suddenly, I saw a bullet-sized tear in the parachute, and then another. I was sure they were shooting at me.

I kicked, swinging the parachute one way and then the other. I wanted to drop faster, straight down, down to the ground.

I took hold of the tangle of ropes rising from one shackle and pulled, tilting the canopy and spilling out air. The chute collapsed, and I fell straight down. I let go of the ropes and the chute filled again. Nobody had taught me this maneuver. I'd read about it in an air force magazine. I collapsed the chute once, and then I did it again.

Now the earth was closer, wide beneath me, like a big brown bowl. Below me were fields and patches of trees, a house on a hill I was drifting straight toward, and a line of high-tension wires.

I tipped the canopy again, spilled the air, and dropped straight down. The ground came up fast. I let go of the ropes, the chute filled, and I smashed down, landing on my hands and knees.

The chute was all around me. Our orders were to bury the chute and try to escape. I started digging in the ground, digging like a dog, clawing at the ground with my fingers, the chute still attached to me. My hands shook violently. I had to hold one hand with the other to get the chute off.

And then two soldiers in blue uniforms appeared over the hill. One had a submachine gun, the other a rifle. Both guns were pointed at me.

I put my hands up. "*Kamerad*," I said. It was the German word for comrade. Friend. It meant "I surrender." I'd read it in a book.

The soldiers were Luftwaffe, German air force. They marched me down the hill to a railroad overpass, where there were a lot of kids, some with guns. The soldiers disarmed me and then led me away from the crowd and into the woods. I thought I was going to be killed. The pits that lined the path looked like graves.

They made me empty my pockets, throw everything on the ground, then take off my coveralls and boots. They took my cigarettes and my Zippo lighter. One of the soldiers cocked his gun.

The trees in the woods were lined in perfect rows. No undergrowth. No place to hide. No place to run. I sat on the ground and waited. The soldier held a gun to my head. I said good-bye to my mother, my father, my girlfriend.

I waited.

On the ground I saw the green GI handkerchief that I used to wipe out the moisture from the inside of my oxygen mask. I pointed to the handkerchief. One of the soldiers nodded, and I took it and put it in my pocket.

So maybe they weren't going to kill me.

They allowed me to dress, then we continued through the woods to the edge of a military airfield. We were somewhere at the outskirts of the city we'd bombed. German fighter planes were lined up along the fence. The soldiers marched me through a gate and into a small office building. It could have been any office, anywhere, except that the two women on the other side of the railing were typing under a picture of Adolf Hitler.

I sat on a bench along a wall. Soldiers came and went, giving the Nazi salute. It was barely noon, maybe a half hour since our plane had entered the bomb run. Was I dreaming? Would I wake up and find it was just a movie? But there were cracks on every wall, even behind Hitler's portrait. Did movies have cracks in the walls?

A German officer, bald and wearing a monocle, who did look like an actor, came up to the railing that separated us and started shouting at me. I stood up. I stood at attention. Time-release bombs exploded outside. He cursed me. He had my wallet in his hand and wanted to know about my plane and where I had flown from. I understood enough German to know what he wanted, but I shook my head as if I understood nothing. I stayed at attention. When he left, I sat down again.

O'Malley was brought in and sat near me. We acted as if we didn't know each other, talking in half phrases and whispers. He had jumped out of the plane after me, then on landing had eluded the Germans, lying flat and crawling through ditches, but finally, they captured him.

"Mike?" I asked. The last time I'd seen him, he was standing in the doorway of the radio compartment.

"He was right behind me," O'Malley said. "Mike jumped." He was sure of that.

"Three chutes," I said, showing him three fingers. "You, me, Young?"

O'Malley shrugged. We sat there, and I smoked all O'Malley's cigarettes. No third man was brought in.

Later, we were taken to a lock-up. There was a peephole in the door of my cell and a pile of straw to sleep on. During the night, soldiers came for us and loaded us on a bus with other captured American fliers, some of them wounded. Mike wasn't among them, nor was there anyone else there from our crew.

The bus moved with dimmed lights to a station, where we got on a train. Sometime later, the train stopped. At the edge of the track an ambulance waited for the wounded.

The rest of us, five American airmen and six armed Luftwaffe guards carrying rifles and rucksacks, set off on foot. From that moment until the end of the war, thirteen days later, we were together, prisoners and guards, constantly on the move.

We walked through the night and into the morning mist. The sun came up and roosters crowed. I was carrying one of our guard's rucksacks as we entered Klattau, a small German-occupied Czech city. We marched down the middle of the street, and from the sidewalks, people cursed and spat at us.

They brought us to a military hospital, where German soldiers, on crutches and in wheelchairs crowded around us. Unlike the civilians outside, they were friendly and wanted to talk. *Alles kaput,* they kept repeating. Everything is done for. The war is lost. They knew they were defeated, that it was only a matter of time. The trick was to stay alive.

That night we were locked in the basement. We could hear the Allied bombardment in the distance, we were that close to the American lines. Had we remained at the hospital, we would have been freed in a day or two. But in the morning, the five of us and our Luftwaffe guards boarded a train that took us south toward Austria and the Austrian Alps, where Hitler had vowed to fight to the death.

Everywhere we went, we were surrounded by retreating German Army units. We hitched rides on their trucks, slept where they slept, ate the food they ate, mostly black bread and cheese, half-rations for the five of us.

I never felt safe. We were strafed, once by Russian fighter planes when we were riding on the back of a truck. In one town, the burgomeister told us to get out as fast as we could, because 50,000 German SS troops were bivouacked there, and he couldn't guarantee our safety.

On May 7, near Linz, Austria, we entered a German Wehrmacht ski troop camp. Our head guard spoke to the camp Kommandant, who had been severely wounded on the Russian front and walked with a cane. Would he take the prisoners? While we stood in a hallway waiting his decision, two Austrian deserters from the German army were brought before him. He sentenced them to be shot the next morning.

The five of us spent the night locked in a classroom, one guard at the door and another outside the window. In the middle of the night, I woke to a commotion outside, excited voices repeating, *Russkie kommen!* The Russians are coming.

The door rattled. Someone said, "To hell with them!"

In the morning, the guards were gone. The door was locked, but the window was open, and we climbed out.

The camp was in turmoil, soldiers rushing every way. No one paid any attention to us. I stopped a passing German soldier. "*Vas ist los?*" What's happening?

"*Alles kaput.*" It's all over.

I pointed to the revolver that he wore in a long leather holster on his waist. "*Bitte.*" Please. If the war was over, could I please have his gun? Without hesitation, he handed it to me. Everything had changed. The war was over. The Germans were defeated. Guns were no use to them anymore.

The five of us stayed close together. We were still surrounded by Germans, with not an American in sight. We found a small disabled car in a garage, and one of our guys, an auto mechanic from Buffalo, New

York, got it started and we all piled in, jammed in. It was a tight squeeze.

The two Austrian deserters who were to be shot that morning wanted to go with us, but there was no room in the car, so they sat on the fenders as we drove out. We were stopped at the gate. "*Amerikaners,*" the Austrians snapped, pointing to us. The German guards saluted, and we drove out.

The road was clogged with German soldiers milling around spilling out into the fields. The ground was littered with the guns they had thrown away. They weren't fighting anymore. Guns could only get them in trouble. It was almost impossible to move. "*Amerikaners, Amerikaners,*" the Austrians kept saying. German officers cleared a path for us. We crept forward.

An American half track came toward us, and we shouted up to them, "Hey!" We banged on the car and called, "We're Americans!" But they drove past us.

On we went, across a broad valley and up into the hills, where we were stopped at a roadblock. American soldiers yanked the Austrians off the fenders. "Turn the goddamn vehicle around and go back!"

We spilled out of the car, yelling "We're Americans! Lucky Strike! New York Yankees! Empire State Building!" The soldiers were part of the Third Army, General Patton's command. We were with our own.

O'Malley and I hugged. We were all crazy with joy.

It was 1945. Thirteen days had passed since our plane had been shot down over Plzen, Czechoslovakia. I was tired. I wanted to eat and sleep. I wanted to get back to our base and get word to my parents that I was alive. And I wanted to find out about Mike and the rest of the crew. Eight of us had been on the plane. Only O'Malley and I were accounted for.

A truckload of GIs on furlough was leaving for Paris. O'Malley and I went with them. The Autobahn, the superhighway through Germany, was full of bomb craters, and there were constant detours. White sheets, flags of surrender, hung from every house. In Munich, I boarded a C-47 for Camp Lucky Strike in France, near Rouen, where all freed POWs were being sent.

With the help of the Red Cross, I sent word to my parents. I later learned that my mother had received the telegram reporting me missing in action on the day the war ended. It was another two weeks before my letter reached her.

When I finally reached to my home base in England, I discovered that our squadron had shipped out, and a new crew occupied our hut. Our plane had been seen falling. Three chutes emerged, before the plane spun out of control, trapping the rest of the crew inside. Who was the third parachutist, and what had happened to him? Nobody knew.

In July, when I was home on leave, I went to see Mike's parents. I didn't want to go. It wasn't me they wanted to see standing there, but they were kind to me. "War is like that," his father said. "Some make it and some don't." Then he left the room.

* * * *

I was young when I went away to the army, a boy leaving home on a great adventure. It was war, and there was danger, but I didn't expect to die. Mike didn't either. We were both sure that, somehow, whatever happened, we'd find a way to survive.

But something had gone wrong. I had survived. I was here and Mike wasn't. I didn't believe that Mike was meant to die or I was meant to live. It was fate, chance, blind luck.

I told the story of that last mission obsessively, trying to explain what could never be explained. Telling the story meant kept Mike and the rest of my crew alive for me.

* * * *

For fifty years I believed that the third parachute was Young, the tail gunner, and that Mike had gone down with the plane.

* * * *

There's another part to this story, a last word, if there is a last word to any story. Not too many years ago, on the fiftieth anniversary of the end of the war in Europe, I was invited back to Plzen, where our plane had gone down. Mirek Kahout, a young Czech, with a fascination for World War II, had done a lot of research and knew all about our plane.

He wrote to me that, immediately after the war, when the Germans were driven out of Czechoslovakia, a memorial had been erected to my crew in a small village, Lidice, outside the city of Plzen. Now, it was to be rededicated. Would I come and speak?

No, I wouldn't come. What was done was done. I didn't visit graves or memorials. Nothing about the trip was sensible. It meant nothing to the dead. Their bodies had been brought home long ago.

But, in the end, I went. Not going felt like abandoning Mike again.

Three young men in jeans and T-shirts were waiting for me at the airport in Prague, all of them wearing the jaunty veteran caps of our own American 398th bomb group: Mirek, his brother Martin, and Kamil, who had borrowed his sister's car to drive us to Plzen. They called themselves SLET, a Czech word that means rally. Mirek spoke a little English. I had memorized a few Czech phrases. *Dobree Dan.* Good morning. *Dyekooyi Vam.* Thank you.

The first thing we did was take pictures. "This is the happiest moment of my life," Mirek said.

We visited the Presidential Palace overlooking Prague and then we drove to the Czech Air Museum, where Mirek showed me a Pratt and Whitney B-17 engine. "From your plane," he said. He pointed to the serial number. "Original research."

From Prague, we drove to Plzen, where, in the cramped apartment he shared with his brother, mother, and grandmother, Mirek had accumulated bits of our plane—a piston, an aluminum panel, even a bent propeller which he kept stored in a backyard shed.

The next day, we drove to a farmer's unplowed field at the edge of the city. "Here, the plane crashed," Mirek said. Using a metal detector, he brought up pieces of our plane that had been in the ground half a century. Pieces of aluminum that looked like molten rock, empty shells, corroded fittings, a fuse, and even some .50 caliber machine gun bullets. Everything he found, he gave me.

He had collected photos taken shortly after the plane crashed. One photo showed a boy in short pants standing on the wing next to the cockpit. The boy had testified that he'd seen a dead man inside the cockpit and even read his dog tags. Halbert—that was the name.

John Halbert was our co-pilot on that mission. He had substituted for Johnny Schmidt, our regular co-pilot, who had been recruited for another mission. It had been John Halbert's first combat mission.

It was a day of revelations. Mirek took me next to a small Catholic cemetery in the middle of a wheat field.

"There," he said, pointing to a stone wall. "Your crew. Buried there." And then, standing on the stone wall, he told me a story about Mike I had never known.

Mike *had* bailed out. He was the third parachutist, and he had landed here. Mirek pointed to the wheat field. Witnesses had seen Mike come down and land safely. They had seen a German military vehicle approach, and a Wehrmacht officer get out holding a revolver. They had seen him shoot and kill Mike.

Mike was buried inside the walled cemetery with the rest of the crew. When the bodies were disinterred to be brought home, all except one were badly burned. One showed a bullet wound.

★ ★ ★ ★

The rededication of the memorial to my crew took place that afternoon. A dusty, hot day. A small gathering. Older people standing in the shade of trees. The marble memorial was smothered in flowers. Plzen is an old city, seven hundred years old that year, a city of memorials. *Nezapomenemei,* the Czechs inscribe on their monuments. *Nezapomenemei.* Never to forget.

When I spoke, I said the names of each of the dead from our crew, where they came from, and how old they were when they died. I thanked the mayor and the people who had come, many of whom had lived through the war. "*Dyekooyi Vam.* Thank you for keeping the memory of my crew alive."

The next day, Mirek and his brother Martin and Martin's girlfriend drove me to the airport. On the way we stopped, and I bought a loaf of rye bread and two bottles of Pilsen beer. Then I flew home. It had been five days and four nights. Hot, dry, summery days. Cool nights in an old Czech hotel with a trolley car outside clattering past every few minutes.

* * * *

Now, when I think about Mike, it's always the bailout I remember, the two of us, our parachutes open, coming down together under a sparkling blue sky.

We landed not that far apart. Alive. Both of us alive.

My fortune was to fall into the hands of the Luftwaffe. Mike's misfortune was to fall into the hands of the Wehrmacht. It could have been the other way around.

The guns we carried in shoulder holsters—did Mike draw his gun, reach for it like the movies? Did he think it was like those war stories we both loved, where at the end, the enemy dead littered the field and the hero stood triumphant? Did he forget that movies were just movies—make-believe stories, not life? After the shoot, when the movie making is done and the lights go on, all the actors get up and go home.

* * * *

When Mike and I went off to war, we had little sense of life except that it was ours, and so was fortune and possibility. I didn't know then, I couldn't have known what I know now—the cold, dumb, skin-of-the-teeth luck that life is.

harry mazer

For over thirty years, veteran author **HARRY MAZER** has been writing books for young people. During World War II, just out of high school and long before he even thought of being a writer, Mazer was part of a B-17 bomber crew, flying combat missions over Germany. On the last mission of that war, his plane was shot down. It was that experience, the need to remember, to tell the story of his crew, that led him finally to becoming a writer. "Join the Army and See the World" is that story.

He and his wife, Norma Fox Mazer, both wanted a family and both wanted to write. During the early years of their marriage, Mazer supported their young family working as a welder and ironworker. At night, while their children slept, they wrote. Of their more than forty-eight books, twenty-eight are by Norma, twenty are by Harry, and three are co-authored: *The Solid Gold Kid* (1977 American Library Association's YASD 100 Best of the Best for Young Adults), *Heartbeat* (1989), and *Bright Days, Stupid Nights* (1992).

Mazer's poignant, gritty writing style is instantly appealing to young readers. He hopes "that my stories will leave readers with the feeling that they've experienced something about life."

The wartime experiences that form the basis of "Join the Army and See the World" also inspired his book *The Last Mission* (1979) and the short story "Till the Day He Died," in *Twelve Shots* (1997), an anthology of gun stories which Mazer edited.

Some recent titles are *The Dog in the Freezer* (1997), *The Wild Kid* (A School Library Journal Best Book of 1998), and *A Boy at War* (2001). Longtime favorites include *Snow Bound* (1987, List of Contemporary Classics, *Booklist*), *The Island Keeper* (1981, A Junior Literary Guild selection), and *Who Is Eddie Leonard?* (1993).

Harry Mazer lives in New York City and Jamesville, New York, with his wife, author Norma Fox Mazer.

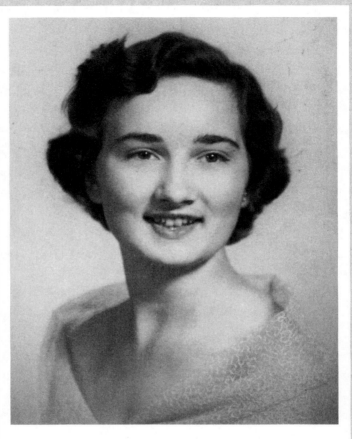

The senior photo from my college yearbook, taken soon after the summer abroad. I'd forgotten about the haircut. I wore my hair long most of my young life.

an innocent abroad—

fragments from the summer of 1953
by KATHERINE PATERSON

THE SUMMER OF 1953 *I was twenty years old and between my junior and senior years at a small college in Tennessee. In England that summer, the young Elizabeth was crowned queen. In the U.S. that summer Ethel and Julius Rosenberg were executed for treason, having been convicted of passing atomic secrets to the Soviets. The case remains controversial, as many people felt the Rosenbergs were victims of the anti-Communist fervor which gripped the country during the 1950s. Thus the placards calling Ike a*

Hitler and an assassin. It was also the summer that the Korean War came to an end.

Earlier that spring I had received a letter from the Presbyterian Church telling of an opportunity for college students to spend a summer working in Europe or Great Britain with organizations and people still trying to recover from the devastation of World War II. The cost to us would be boat fare (a wartime troopship only slightly converted) and whatever traveling we wished to do on our own. The local hosts would provide room and board while we were working.

Vesta, a close friend who was studying French, applied to go to work in a French camp for children. I, an English major, applied to work in a small church which had just been built on a new housing development outside of Bristol, England. We were both accepted. We decided to spend two weeks traveling before we went to our separate assignments. That we were young, idealistic, and naive goes without saying.

The record of this summer which profoundly changed my life is in the letters that I wrote home. Here, greatly abridged, is that record, beginning with June 21, 1953, which was my parents' thirtieth wedding anniversary, and ending just before their birthdays, which were September 6 and 7.

✦ ✦ ✦ ✦

June 21

Dear Ones,

Father's Day plus thirty years hard labor have made this quite a *jour de fête*. Really, even many miles and five hours different away, the knowing of you sweet ones glows away in my heart.

We debarked about nine and went through customs in a hurry. There was a bus to take us to the station. Vesta and I checked our bags and bought our third-class tickets and wandered around the city until time for the Paris train. I bought a pair of gloves which I needed from a lady in a tall lace hat from Brittany. She had crocheted them.

Perhaps the most unhappy impression of France is the quantity of signs that read *"Sauver les Rosenbergs!"* And then the sequel: *"Ike Assassin! Hitler!"* There have been demonstrations all over the city. Friday night we walked down the Champs Elysées to the Arc de Triomphe. We heard a group of young men talking excitedly together but didn't know what was going on. Then sitting quietly beneath the Arc, we were startled when a large group of mostly young adults leaped to their feet and sang beautifully, but with frightening fervor, "The Marseillaise." Then, chanting something unrecognizable, they marched down the avenue.

I was consumed with curiosity, so I asked a nearby policeman in my best brand of American French, why the demonstration. He smiled slightly and shrugged. "*Je ne sais pas.*" Are they students? I knew that at [the height of summer] the university students tended to go on a rampage. "*Peut-être.*" We read in the paper the next day that the Rosenbergs had finally been executed.

I have seen a little of what makes Paris beloved. It's romantic, but in a real sense, equally artificial. The Notre-Dame stained glass and the Louvre's Winged Victory were the two things that made me breathe more rapidly. We climbed the Eiffel Tower and watched the streets crawling with traffic. What a ghastly mess. I've been tempted more than once to catch the Métro, go one block, cross the street underground, and ride back a block in order to avoid crossing the actual street. Usually Vesta and I just grab hold of each other, look straight ahead, and keep moving.

Saturday night we saw *Aida* at the opera. We were late getting tickets so we sat way to the side on the *troisième*. By standing up and breathing down the necks of the gentleman and lady in front of us in our box (just like the movies!) we could see a good three fourths of the stage.

We're now on the train to Switzerland. We decided to skip Geneva–we're tired of cities and tourists—and go to Frutigen which is in the middle of nowhere.

June 22
The is the closest place to heaven I've been. My first

impression of Switzerland was train stations with red geraniums in their windowboxes. Then we got into the mountains and lakes. I haven't quite recovered.

Frau Seiber who runs our tiny hotel speaks English fairly well. I called her from the station. "Vere are you? At ze station? I come get you!" I protested. "No, no, no, I come." She came and walked us up the street, across the leaping mountain stream, and around the corner to her and her husband's (he's a pastry cook as my added pounds will soon testify) pension.

Frutigen is the place where you long for everyone you love to help drink in the excess of beauty, the overpowering variety of snow-capped mountains, and of quaint beauty of flower boxes and chalets. Vesta and I are coming back on our honeymoons or to write our books, we haven't quite decided which.

June 24

If you have construed a mental image of Vesta and me scaling the side of a glacier in the footsteps of a leather-breeched guide, you can forget it. Today we got the closest we'll get to it, and that's not very close.

Frau Seiber packed us a lunch of ham buns, hard-boiled eggs, oranges, and patisseries. We caught the train to Kanderstag. Then we walked for about twelve minutes to a chairlift. The thought of riding a chairlift had given me uneasiness to the tummy previously, but actually it was rather tame and thoroughly enjoyable. After the chairlift we walked for about twenty minutes to the Blue Lake. It's really a beautiful greenish lake right in the midst of snow-capped mountains. There are scores of waterfalls coming into it from the melting snows above. It was a little cloudy when we got there, but we found ourselves a big flat rock over the lake and ate our lunch.

Vesta teased me about my "girl guide spirit" because I insisted that we take a side path down the mountain rather than the main one. The walk was beautiful. We were right amongst the pine trees, crossing little streams and looking up at the ever-present mountains. Every tiny chalet near the timber line looks like the alm-uncle's home, and all the little girls like Heidis. I wish you could see these people. They have magnificent faces—rosy cheeked and open faced. I love the mustached, pipe-smoking old men dressed in their short pants and riding their bicycles. Everybody in Europe has a bicycle, whether they're six or eighty-five. The little old ladies zooming around tickle me more than anything.

July 1

It rained the last day in Frutigen so I never got the colored pictures. That evening after Frau Seiber had given us a big early supper, she walked with us to the station and saw us off. Vesta and I were very touched, feeling almost as though we'd left home twice in one month.

The scenery from Frutigen until nightfall was achingly beautiful. It seemed that the frequent tunnels were a necessary safeguard against fairly bursting from all the majesty of it. The tiny villages trustingly cuddled on the knees of the hoary-haired mountains—the rivers lined by straight rows of poplars—all of it appearing as toyland from our train window except the giant hills in the background.

It would be impossible to tell of Florence without including Julian. We didn't meet him on the train, for he sat across from us with his whole being concentrated upon a gigantic volume which turned out to be an Italian text on international law.

When we got up to leave the train at Florence, so did he. In fact he took Vesta's bag off the train in a gentlemanly fashion and then smiled and departed.

It was about 5:30 A.M. which made us hesitate about going straight to the hotel. Julian must have thought we were lost, for he suddenly reappeared and offered to get us a hotel. Being Victorianly suspicious, I politely clammed up with the reply that we already had one. Before I knew it Vesta had produced the address, and Julian (as he later introduced himself) was escorting us to it.

He was very polite. He was a student at the University of Florence, and he was taking big exams beginning that day for his doctorate in political science. Frankly, my mind was rather busy trying to decide what on earth Mother would think, but we got very safely to our destination and waved him good-bye.

At six we were sitting on the stairs eating our bread and cheese breakfast, wondering whether to knock or not. Finally, at about quarter to seven we knocked. It was very apparent that our host was not long out of bed when he finally answered.

Nevertheless, we took a nap and spent the morning at the Pitti Palace, the old hangout of the Medicis. It is now a fabulous art gallery with gardens. We gazed at Raphael's *Madonna of the Bed* and were generally awestruck by intricate mosaics and gilded ceilings.

By lunchtime the effects of our all-night trip were beginning to show despite our constant consumption of malted milk tablets, so we divided the afternoon between the bed, a necessary trip to American Express, and a look at some of the enchanting shops.

We had determined earlier to spend our only evening in Florence taking a bus ride up Michelangelo Hill and looking over the city. We were just looking for the bus stop when up ran Julian. He was gladder to see us than we him. Vesta had repented her early innocence and we were both quite cool, but he wasn't to be dampened by convention-bound foreigners. In enthusiastic, if broken, English, he personally escorted us to the bus and up to the hill.

Bit by bit we learned that he was Jewish, that he had spent a year in Dachau, that his parents had become Methodists, but he was still very loyally and quite orthodoxically Jewish, that he had worked in Israel in some minor connection with Ralph Bunche, that he hated Germans, that he really didn't want to, but thought he couldn't help it, that his sister was a research chemist and his two brothers importers. He was really a fascinating, unusual person and a little bit lonely.

We walked about the city a bit and when he left us, he said: "Please do not offend me to have breakfast with me." By this time, even my suspicions were gone, so we met him at 8:30. After breakfast, he took us to the Uffizi. He knew a great deal about art and especially these galleries, so it was much better than a guided tour. He showed us the spot on the bridge where Dante first saw Beatrice. He showed us the golden chapel doors which Michelangelo said were fit to be the doors of Paradise. Finally, at twelve, we parted—he to his exam and we to our train. I'm really grateful for getting to know Florence just that way in spite of all my (and your) objections to speaking to strange men who are not in uniform.

On Monday Vesta and I parted, not without a tear, and with the channel on very good behavior I soon found myself amongst this happy breed of men. The boat train got into London at a little after six. I called my friends from the station, only to find that they were in Oxford for the day and wouldn't return until late. After some hesitation ("This isn't a hostel, you know") the housekeeper at Marnham House gave me the directions via tube and trolley to London's East End.

The next morning I was off to Bristol. I made the happy mistake of riding the bus all the way to the station. Happy because I saw many of the Coronation remains, the hanging crown, Trafalgar Square, the equestrian statue of the queen—mistake because it took longer than I figured. Miraculously enough, a lovely lady appeared, helped me with my bags, watched them while I went to get a ticket, saw me off on the train. I'd never have made it without her. By the way, I spent Independence Day seeing the technicolor movie, *A Queen Is Crowned*.

July 5

The Swiss are the best people in the world next to the English. I got out of the train compartment and standing almost directly in front of me was a tall young man in a clerical collar. His hair was sort of sandy and his smile quite friendly, and I knew in a moment it must be Michael Whitehorn. We rode the bus to the center of Bristol where the gardens still wear their charming coronation crown and transferred to a Lockleaze bus. Lockleaze is a housing project on the edge of town. The church, which is quite new, is sort of in the middle. There are about five thousand people in Lockleaze, poor, but not actually poverty-stricken (my own observation thus far). Mrs. Whitehorn (Margaret) came downstairs from the manse (it's above the Sunday School) to greet us. She's slender, prematurely gray, charmingly British, with a dimple in her chin. Sheila, the baby, was in bed, and high tea was on the table, so we ate. Miss Pash, the parish assistant, was up after supper. She lives next door. She's short, a little plump, with the "jolliest" face and eyes and temperament to match. The "cold British," phooey.

The first person I saw this morning was Sheila. Huge blue eyes, curly hair, wide smile, and (get this) a dimple in her nose. She's fourteen months and perfectly fat and precious.

At 9:30 Michael, Miss Pash, about 160 children, and scattered parents and I got on four busses and went to the country. It rained some, but we had a marvelous time with cricket (for the boys) and rounders ("depraved baseball" according to Michael, for the girls). We had lunch at twelve with races afterward and tea at five, and I mean tea. We gathered for tea in a borrowed hall nearby. Everybody had a cup, and milk, tea, and sugar came round for all followed by mounds of sandwiches, buns, and all sorts of cake.

I was given the honor of awarding the prizes to the winners of the races, even got a prize myself, a little box of chocolates, which, I hasten to say, weren't earned.

The children are more fun than anything and sound so educated to me. The adults are wonderfully friendly, eager to talk about America, the Americans they've known, friends in the service, etc. The war is almost forgotten, not quite. Bristol was hit pretty badly, and you can see empty spots still, even though the rubbish is cleared.

July 9

Today I've been taking Miss Pash's place at two school trips. This morning I helped chaperone Miss Brown's five-year-olds on a trip to the aerodrome to watch the planes. This afternoon Miss Bovey's "just sevens" went to a really picturesque old English farm to see the milking. They used machines. Quite a contrast to the old stone barn.

Tomorrow more visiting, an interview from one of the local newspapers, Brownies in the evening. Saturday I have an invitation to go to Weston Beach with the Phillipses. They have one little girl, Alison aged five, who remarked at Communion last Sunday when the bread was passed: "Wait a minute, Mummy, and they'll bring you the butter."

Tuesday the Whitehorns left for Stratford. Miss

Pash and I felt a little let down when the taxi pulled away, but she's been keeping me comforted with stacks of scones, literally gallons of tea.

I'm slated to meet the lord mayor of Bristol next Wednesday at a modern school prize giving—strictly informally, but it does sound "posh." Rath*er.*

July 16

Sunday morning I "preached" my first sermon at the youth service. It's not all young people, but mostly. I was robed in Miss Pash's mantle, and everything was all right except in announcing the responsive readings I spoke too quickly and they had a job figuring out what I said.

Right now I'm in Aston Cantlow with the Whitehorns. This is a village near Stratford where Shakespeare's parents were married. Last night Margaret and two cousins with a car took me to see *The Merchant of Venice*. What acting! Michael Redgrave, one of the top British actors, portrayed a fawning, yet proud Shylock.

Sheila is just beginning to walk.

July 31

Things keep blossoming and days swim by, and still you wait in vain for a letter.

Shall I start with the conference? It was the annual General Conference of the Student Christian

Movement of Great Britain and Ireland—380 students including about 45 overseas students, 6 of whom were Americans. I am greatly impressed by English and Scottish students—sincerity and wit are the two words that come to mind.

The theme of the conference was Peace. It seemed quite fitting that news of the armistice should come on Sunday. The people over here, however, are surprisingly cut off from Korea. To them it's another area of unrest. With Malaya and South Africa continually on their minds as well, the Korean War's end was a relief but not a respite from fighting.

The attitude of many British people toward world affairs was a new thing to me altogether. The general feeling seems to be that there are at present two strong powers almost evenly matched. Great Britain's place in the world is to ease as best as possible the terrific global tension between Russia and the U.S. They have allied themselves with us, but if we get any crazy ideas, they're sure to tell us that we can "jolly well go it alone." The American soldier and tourist have damaged Anglo-American relationships beyond belief, second only in this respect to American movies. In the conference this came out in talks, discussions, and good-natured kidding, but it set us six Americans to serious thinking. On Saturday night three of us overseas students had a chance to speak. One was a German boy from the Eastern zone, another was a

Nigerian boy, and I was the American. It seemed that I should say that we American Christians are interested in the rest of the world for more than just their potential military value. I was surprised and quite warmed by the response.

The day after the conference ended I drove down to Cambridge with some folks who live there. The Whitehorns were there visiting his parents. Michael, Margaret, Sheila, and I went punting on the river at the "backs." One punts by standing on a platform at the end of a long boat and pushing a tall pole in the water and trusting you won't fall off. I didn't, but I might have once or twice.

August 24

Sunday I took charge of the Beginner's Class again. They were lively as usual. Despite one little girl's spilling the cup of paste all over her woolen skirt and the free entertainment by several of our more precocious, we somehow made it through.

September 2

Little St. James and I have grown up a lot this summer. I was in Lockleaze for her first wedding and her first funeral. One of our guides and Sunday School helpers, Pat Adams, who was fourteen, fell from a tree she was climbing and died soon afterwards. The last time I saw her was at Girl Guides the Friday night before her death. She and a couple of the other young live wires had given me quite a run for my money. It was hard to believe.

The little church was packed, mostly with her young friends. They sang like angels, bless them. Even the parents were singing before the service was over. Michael spoke like an inspired one that he is. It seemed strange that after all the happiness I have known there, that service would be my last afternoon in Lockleaze.

It seems a shame that I shall be tossing on the sea when I ought to be celebrating your birthdays with you. At first I wondered why I hadn't planned to get back earlier, but I think the wise Lord kept me here for Pat's death.

Remind me to tell you of all the people I have known here, including precious old deaf Mr. Gavin who comes to church anyway, although he's often left singing the last phrase alone; little Christine who looks like the Brownie elf she is; Mrs. Rylett with four young sons and prospects of twins, always full of cheer; Mrs. Marshall, who's neurotic and confused; Christopher with sparkling black eyes; Mr. Harris, the tubby organist who teases Americans; Mrs. Ginter with the lovely mind who cleans the church to make ends meet; Vivien and Pat, who were too shy to give me a snapshot of themselves, so made Pat's little sister do it for them; Edwin Willis, who almost behaved himself in Sunday School last Sunday for the first time. Cheryl with intelligence; and Christine with the charming freckles. All of these join me in wishing you birthdays full of joy.

The boat lands Sunday the thirteenth. On Monday I'll try to wire what time I'll get to Washington.

Your,
K.

katherine paterson

KATHERINE PATERSON did not always want to be a writer. She confesses, "When I was ten, I wanted to be either a movie star or a missionary. When I was twenty, I wanted to get married and have lots of children."

In between dreams, Paterson studied at King College in Bristol, Tennessee, where she spent the majority of her time reading English and American literature. She later taught at a rural school in northern Virginia—where "almost all my children were like Jesse Aarons" from her book *Bridge to Terabithia*.

Pursuing her missionary dream, Paterson studied Bible and Christian education in graduate school in Richmond, Virginia, and hoped to go to China. But as she explains, "China was closed to Americans in 1957, and a Japanese friend urged me to go to Japan instead."

For four years Paterson happily lived and worked among the Japanese—with whom she thought she would spend her life. "But when I returned to the States for a year of study in New York," she reveals, "I met a young Presbyterian pastor who changed the direction of my life once again." They married, and soon Paterson fulfilled her dream of having lots of children.

It is then that she eventually began writing. A church friend took her to a creative writing course—

and after some time the novel she wrote in that course was published. Paterson's books have earned her two Newbery medals, for *Bridge to Terabithia* (1978) and *Jacob Have I Loved* (1981), two National Book awards, for *The Master Puppeteer* (1977) and *The Great Gilly Hopkins* (1979), a Boston Globe-Horn Book Picture Book Award for *The Tale of the Mandarin Ducks* (1990), and many other accolades. Her most recent books are *The Invisible Child: On Reading and Writing Books for Children* (2001) and *The Same Stuff as Stars* (2002).

She remembers the summer of 1953 described in "An Innocent Abroad" as a turning point in the way she viewed the world. Although she had lived in China as a child, it wasn't until that summer that she became aware of the ways the rest of the world looked at the United States, certainly with gratitude for U.S. help in World War II but also with resentment. Many people in Europe thought that the United States was rich and arrogant and had trouble understanding the U.S. paranoia regarding the Communist countries.

At the end of that summer abroad, the sudden death of a child in Bristol was an ominous foreshadowing of the death of Lisa Hill, a young friend of her son, who, many years later, inspired the writing of *Bridge to Terabithia*.

Paterson currently lives in Barre, Vermont, and has four children and seven grandchildren.

One sticky day, my father spotted these men selling
fruits and vegetables from their licensed one-horse
cart. I jumped out of the car to get cantaloupes. I
hated to wear shoes, and my parents never made me.

looking for america
by ELIZABETH PARTRIDGE

WHAT I HATED MOST was how people stared at us. I didn't mind so much while we were driving, and I would see people's mouths drop open as we flew by. But I hated it when we pulled into a campground or a gas station. As soon as my father rolled down the window, someone would stick his head in, look us over, and ask, "Where're you folks from?"

"California," my dad would say. They'd nod, like that explained it.

But it didn't, of course. It didn't begin to explain

why our family was driving across the country in the summer of 1963, in an old Cadillac limousine painted a bright, metallic gold. The five of us kids didn't sit tidily in a row like regular kids but instead were sprawled on a double bed mattress that my dad had spread across the back. My parents called it "looking for America." I thought it was more like being looked *at* by America.

My dad was a freelance photographer, and to fund our trip he'd arranged to photograph buildings and parks all over the United States. We ranged in age from my seventeen-year-old sister, Joan, to baby Aaron. I was eleven, smack in the middle of the pack, with my brother Josh three years older and my sister Meg two years younger.

We threaded our way through national and state parks, zigzagging toward New York City. In the Southwest we climbed rickety wooden ladders up a cliff into old Pueblo Indian houses; in Yellowstone we were drenched by Old Faithful; in Kansas we rolled out of bed at five A.M. to watch a farmer milk his cows.

"Look at it!" my father would say, throwing his arms out. "Just look at it all." With off-the-cuff comments by my father, and more thoughtful views from my mother, we took in the rhythms and lives of other Americans. "We're lucky to be alive," my father said. "Right now, right here!"

By late August we had made it to New York, camped our way down the Great Smoky Mountains, and were headed for Atlanta, Georgia.

An architect my father knew, Mr. McNeeley, had designed his own house in Atlanta. We were invited to stay while my father photographed the house. I was excited—after weeks of smoky fires and pit toilets, we were going to stay in a real house. Maybe they'd even have a TV in their rumpus room and we could spread out on a comfortable couch and watch something like *The Wonderful World of Disney*.

We hit the Deep South just as a hot spell struck. The air was thick and steamy and smelled like mildew. The buzz of cicadas filled my ears.

My mother insisted we stop for the night at a campground outside of Atlanta, so we could clean up. After dinner she handed out towels and shepherded us into the public showers, a squat cement building with huge spiders in the corners and black beetles scuttling across the wet floors. Washing my hair, I discovered a big knotted tangle in the back, but it hurt too much when I tried to brush it out so I just left it. At least my hair was clean.

Late the next morning when we arrived at the McNeeley's, I saw that my mother had been right to tidy us up. Their new house was perfect. Every surface was shiny clean, nothing out of place. Built around a courtyard filled with plants, floor to ceiling glass windows let a dappled green light into every room. Antique Persian rugs covered the smooth cement floors, and modern sculptures made of glass and ceramic perched on back-lit shelves. There wasn't a rumpus room in sight. Mrs. McNeely wore bright red lipstick and white slacks with a crisp linen blouse. I was painfully aware of the big snarl in my hair.

Mrs. McNeeley showed my sisters and me into a guest room with its own bathroom loaded with huge, fluffy towels and sweet-smelling soap, then left us, saying she needed to speak with the cook about lunch arrangements.

I stood on one foot and stared out into the courtyard. Our mother was right to be concerned: we didn't fit in. "How long do you think we're staying here?" I asked Meg nervously.

At lunchtime my mother beckoned me to take the chair next to Aaron. A tall black woman wearing a starched apron came in through a swinging door. She carried a casserole with a heavy silver spoon laid across the top.

"Thank you, Annie," said Mrs. McNeeley. I stared at my mother, frozen. What were we supposed to do now? Did we dip the spoon in the casserole and serve ourselves? Did we get served? Annie stood next to my mother, the casserole in her outstretched arms. My mother looked uncomfortable and busied herself with tucking a napkin into the neck of Aaron's shirt. My stomach twisted. Even my mother wasn't sure what to do.

"Please," said Mrs. McNeeley to my mother, "help yourself."

When Annie stood next to me I just looked at her helplessly, afraid I would spill casserole all over my lap from the big silver spoon. She winked at me so quickly I wasn't sure she had, and put a spoonful of casserole on my plate.

After lunch my father started shooting interiors of the house. The rest of us were shepherded to the courtyard. My mother and Mrs. McNeeley sat under a big umbrella, and Annie brought out a pitcher of iced tea and tall glasses full of clinking ice cubes.

Meg and I played hopscotch on the flagstones, while Joan challenged Josh to a game of rummy. Aaron sat and banged on a metal pail. The heat fell down on us, heavy and moist, and the whiny buzz of the cicadas set my teeth on edge. Aaron smashed his hand under the pail and started screaming. Suddenly my head felt like it was exploding with noise and heat and an anxious worry.

I had to get away from my sisters and brothers, away from Mrs. McNeeley sitting stiffly with a tight smile. I slipped inside, crossed the dining room, and bolted through the swinging door, right into the kitchen. Annie stood with her back to me, working at the sink.

"Yes, Ma'am?" she said, turning around. "Oh," she said, surprised to see me. I stood awkwardly, ready to dash out again. Maybe I wasn't allowed in the kitchen. The cook tipped her head toward a small pine table.

"Sit, honey," she said. I tried to ease graciously into the chair but managed to knock my funny bone on the edge of the table and let out a yelp.

"You must be growing," the cook said. "Skinny as all get out, and don't know where your body's at."

I didn't want to tell her I was always banging myself on something. She put two sugar cookies and a tall, cold glass of milk in front of me. As I ate, I watched her wash the lunch dishes. Steam rose from the sink, and moisture beaded up on her forehead. When she finished she filled a quart-size canning jar with cold water and drank. I was grateful for her quiet company.

When Aaron woke up from his nap we walked to a nearby city park. Though the sun was low, the air still felt like we were walking in a huge oven, with more heat radiating up from the cement. My mother sat on a bench next to the sandbox and plunked Aaron down in the sand.

I spotted a drinking fountain and ran over, guzzling the water in great big gulps. Meg thumped into my back.

"My turn!" she said. I clung tight to the faucet and

jabbed backward at her with my elbows until my stomach was full.

When I stood up, water slid down my neck and under my shirt. Over the fountain was a sign I hadn't noticed: "Whites Only."

"Mom," I yelled back across the playground. "What does 'Whites Only' mean?"

My mother flung her hand out. "Sh. . . ." she said. "Come over here."

I stood next to my mother, who leaned in close. "Negroes aren't allowed to drink from the same fountains as whites in the South, or use the same bathrooms."

I stared at my mother, disbelieving.

"Are those rules?"

"More than rules," she said sadly. "Laws."

I walked all around the playground, but I didn't see any other drinking fountain.

* * * *

The next morning as my parents were packing the car, I slipped back into the kitchen.

"We're leaving," I said to Annie.

"I know, honey," she said. "You have a good trip now, you hear?"

The breakfast dishes were sitting in the rack drying, carrots and potatoes lay on the counter, next to her half-full jar of water. I wanted to ask Annie what she did when she got thirsty at the park. But it seemed like too big a question. I searched for something I could ask, something that was small and not tangled up.

"Why do you drink from a jar?" I blurted out.

She looked at me, considering. Her eyes were full of a lot of things I couldn't read.

"I get mighty thirsty," she finally said. "Those glasses aren't big enough for me."

I didn't understand. She was by the sink all day where she could easily refill her glass.

I heard my father call out, "Let's go!" and I spun out of the kitchen through the swinging door. We drove away from the house of clean rooms and dappled green light and extra-good behavior. Away from the park and kitchen and rules—laws—I didn't understand.

In no time we were out on the highway, my father whistling with the joy of being back on the open road. I leaned over the front seat and asked my mother, "Why did Annie drink out of a jar?"

My mother didn't look at me but spoke softly to her hands resting in her lap. "She probably wasn't allowed to drink from the glasses the family used."

I lay back on the mattress and thought about that. The cook prepared all their food, washing, peeling, chopping, and serving. She set the table, touching every dish. Why couldn't she drink out of their glasses?

My mother must have felt me thinking behind her,

because she turned around and said gently, "Some things just don't make sense."

She turned back, discomfort settling on her shoulders like an old sorrow. It was all too big, too complicated, even for her.

I still didn't understand. Why would everyone go along with something that didn't make any sense? I rolled down my window and let the hot air buffet my face, hoping it would blow away some of the helplessness I felt.

elizabeth partridge

Remembering the trip described in "Looking for America," **ELIZABETH PARTRIDGE** reflects: "Ever since I cracked the reading code, I've been an avid reader, going to the library every week and checking out armloads of books. (I still do.) On our trip across America in 1963 I had no library, and no books. I consoled myself by reading signs—advertising, street signs, anything I could find.

"The sign I remember most poignantly was hanging over a drinking fountain: 'Whites Only.' There was so much wrapped up in those two words that I couldn't fathom. I was a big believer in fairness (I still am) and this was unbelievably unfair, and tangled up with a lot of things I didn't understand. The most incomprehensible part was that everyone seemed to be going along with it—both whites and blacks.

"But change was coming, and coming fast. On August 28, 1963, while we had been driving down the Great Smoky Mountains, Martin Luther King Jr. stood on the steps of the Lincoln Memorial in Washington D.C. giving his famous speech, 'I Have a Dream.'

I have a dream that one day even the state of Mississippi, a desert state, sweltering with the heat of injustice and oppression, will be transformed into an oasis of freedom and justice.

I have a dream that my four children will one day live in a nation where they will not be judged by the color of their skin but by the content of their character. I have a dream today.

"This was decades ago, but I still wonder if Annie heard Martin Luther King Jr.'s speech on the radio, or read it in the paper. Did she talk with her family and friends about it? What were all those unspoken thoughts and feelings I glimpsed in her eyes? How did her life change with the Civil Rights Movement?"

Elizabeth Partridge grew up in a family of photographers, including her grandmother, Imogen Cunningham, and her godmother, Dorothea Lange. In 1974, Partridge was the first student to graduate with a Women's Studies degree from the University of California at Berkeley. A year later she went to Great Britain where she studied Chinese medicine and earned a Licentiate of Acupuncture in 1978.

When Partridge returned from England, she set up a medical practice using acupuncture and herbal medicine, married, and had two sons. Later she began writing books for children and adults. Among her recent titles are the picture book *Moon Glowing* (2002) and the 2002 National Book Award nominee *This Land Was Made for You and Me: The Life and Songs of Woody Guthrie*.

It may look like it's circa 1932, but no, I'm afraid this photo was taken in 1991, shortly before I graduated from college.

a brief guide to the ghosts of great britain
by M. T. ANDERSON

i.

IT WAS NIGHT; my parents, my little sister, and I were driving through the bare, dark hills of Scotland, looking for a place to stay. We had assumed that we would hit a town where we could find a restaurant and a bed and breakfast. Instead, nothing but hills, heather, moors, and sloppy cairns.

I was seventeen and was heading off to spend a year in a boarding school in the south of England. I had gotten to this point by watching too much public television. Worse, following that, I had read too many

English novels, the ones where beautiful women the color of Brie fell in love with beautiful men the color of bread mold; the ones where people felt quiet longing and sorrow on the lawns of country houses; the books where dissipated noblewomen revenged themselves on their husbands through fatal schemes involving mercury sublimate and the Victrola. I found it all riveting. So, having no other direction, I was off to an English boarding school. We were smack in the middle of the middle class, so this kind of thing was unheard of for us, and exciting. My parents had decided to come over with me to Britain for a vacation before my school term started. We had done pretty well finding places to stay by just driving and taking what came.

What came on that particular evening was an isolated B&B/restaurant, lit up with red lanterns on a bleak stretch of winding road. It was called Food among the Pines. I could not help but picture a carcass hung in a tree. We laughed a little about the red lights when we pulled in.

The entrance hall was hung with dark velvet. For service, one had to strike a gong hung between ram's horns. A young man slipped out from between the folds of velvet. He made a reservation for us in the dining room, and took us up to the place's two bedrooms, one for my parents, one for my little sister and me.

The bedrooms were unusual. The mirrors had been underlaid with purple and green sparkles. The clocks' faces had been taken out and replaced with flowers. On the mantelpiece were leather-bound books about levitation, demonology, and the coming of decay. On the walls were landscapes that looked like they had been painted in a delirium.

My sister was only seven, and just wanted to sleep. We left her in the room. I noticed that my mother checked the door three times to see that it was securely locked.

We went down to dinner.

Half the dining room was painted white, and half was painted black. In a niche, there was a statue of the horned god Pan dancing. There were oil pictures on the walls of nautical disasters, ships going down. Most of the tables were full. While we ate, a woman at the table next to us sobbed and would not stop.

This was beyond our ken. We were Americans. We were suburban. Good Lord, we were Episcopalians. I couldn't help but picture the waiter bringing out my sister baked and blackened on a platter, gagged with an apple.

"I think," said my father, "that you two are taking this all a little too far."

That seemed likely. We ate our dinner. I had the chicken Kiev.

Finally, we finished. When we stood up, all conversation in the restaurant ceased. All the other guests turned to us. They waved. They all smiled.

They all said, together, "Good night."

We went to our rooms. We locked ourselves in.

At eleven forty-five, all of the guests left the dining room. Twenty or so of them. They walked back into the woods. The night was black.

At twelve fifteen, they returned. Whatever ritual they performed in the forest at midnight was now complete. They got into their cars and drove away.

The next morning, I opted to skip the fresh bacon.

We went out to our car, past a shop that we now saw was connected to the restaurant, a wizardry supply store.

I was shaking with excitement. Here I was. Where I wanted to be—a place with cults, with ghosts, with shops that sold wands. In America, I hadn't been living. I had just been reading. Now I was ready to start to live. I imagined that Britain was a place of secret passages and midnight trysts by candlelight, dark Jacobean paneling and medieval crypts.

And I was ready for it all.

ii.

It is said that at Mannington Hall, an undead priest stands by the fire in robes of silk. At Hinton Ampner, footsteps tread up and down the passages, and doors slam by themselves. At Borley Rectory, a headless man wanders the gardens, a nun weeps on the walk, voices whisper warnings, and a black coach flies through the hedges and walls. An unspeakable and inhuman Thing

inhabited a room at No. 50 Berkeley Square in London;
whoever saw it died of terror or went stark, raving mad.
On the Isle of Man, a family was haunted for many
years by a talking, singing mongoose named Gef.

iii.

In America, I was a nerd. I read books about great
deeds and love affairs and great crimes in great houses—
assassins skulking down cobbled streets—quite a few
about men waving spears at dragons in the midst of
the pampas grass—but I myself was knock-kneed and
gawky; my pants were generally too tight and too
short. I didn't know how to comb my hair, so I just
scraped it straight back and then wore a hat crushed
over it to flatten it. My glasses were square, and their
light-sensitive lenses had somehow malfunctioned
chemically, making them continually a drug-dealer
gray. I had a pair of jeans with orange stitching. I
walked with a stoop to obscure my height.

I lived in the library. I played role-playing games in
which it was the Middle Ages and I was potent with
magic, or games where it was the Roaring Twenties
and everyone was witty and fabulous and English and
threatened by fish gods. My friends and I did not like
being nerds—it didn't make sense to us, and we
noticed we still didn't do too well in science—but however ill-fitting, that was the only image available to us.

When I decided to go to England, it was because I

was tired of who I had to be in America. From everything I read, things in England seemed more exciting. I didn't know why, but most of the intelligent adults I knew were Anglophiles. There, I thought, is where the adventure is. There, I thought, is a land where eccentricity thrives. It's a country where people listen to string quartets. I had never listened to a string quartet myself, but it seemed like a good idea. There, I thought, they love Shakespeare. There I will not get my ass kicked for reading *Beowulf*. It is a *realm*, I thought, a realm—one that is cultured and vivid.

England is strangely compelling to Americans. Though we may rarely think of it, it is a potent land for us still in the geography of national fantasy. We are a nation that was once a colony. We are still infested with the English dead. We can defy them all we want; but when, for example, we portray the English in films, they are either godlike or monstrous. They are never simply human. They remain, in some way, the image of the overlord, set against our simplicity.

Their kingdom seemed to me like a wonderland, a promise of magic, a chance to shake a ghost by the hand.

And so I began my lesson in nation and image.

iv.

Unfortunately, nothing about boarding school proved my sense of Britain wrong. We were on the outskirts of town—a series of cloisters and turrets spread across the meadows. Some of the boys had to wear black robes. Up above the school, there was a hill with a prehistoric stone maze. King Arthur's Round Table was hanging in the town hall—or a forgery that people called by that name.

There were secret passages, in the sense that when we slipped out of our boarding houses after nine, we had to use elaborate routes, knowing which windows could be jimmied, which walls offered purchase, which rain gutters were bracketed securely. We were aware of our roles as aspiring artists and aesthetical snots at an English boarding school. We put on a Cubist drama involving percussion music and lots of cabbages. We listened to Requiem masses. We broke into construction sites and had black-tie functions there, sitting on girders over huge gulfs.

It was just what I had been longing for—just what I couldn't find in America: a place where it was not considered shameful to enjoy learning. Where I didn't have to hide the fact that I liked studying Elizabethan drama, say, or medieval history, which I now studied for hours a day, before we slipped over the walls after roll call, and went out to the pubs, or went off to play our pranks—tying together everything in someone's room with string, or having shaving foam fights in an old bomb shelter, or even just enjoying the simple pleasure of spreading Saran wrap over toilet-bowls.

One night my friend Hugh and I decided to disguise

ourselves and follow this girl he had a crush on to find out where she lived. It was not a great plan. We waited until seven, when she got off work. I disguised myself as the reddleman from Thomas Hardy's *The Return of the Native*, and Hugh disguised himself as Geppetto the toymaker. It wasn't long before we had to take evasive action.

Hugh took me down a lane I'd never been down before. There was an old monastery there. There was a storm coming. The clouds were thick and dark. We could hardly see as we stumbled past old tombs, down to a river.

We sat there and drank something foul called Organic Scrumpie. We talked about the girl. The wind was getting wilder and wilder. The rain had started falling. There was a swan on the black water. Everything looked exactly as it should. Above us, against the dirty light of the town, we could see the hill with its sacred grove and its neolithic stone maze.

"*Panta rei,*" said Hugh, who was studying Greek, and drunk. "Everything is in flux." He spat something and looked around. "It's supposed to be haunted, this place. Some kid who hung himself."

"Why?" I asked.

"They say he was homosexual. That's not it, actually. He was a vegetarian. Then he heard that plants felt pain, too. So it was hang or starve."

I started laughing as the clouds turned in circles

above me, and the water churned in eddies below me, and the swan swam, and the monastery was dark behind us. I said, "Gothic." I was unsteady on my feet. I said, "This—it's living! I'm living!" I pointed at the graveyard. *"So I want the ghost! Bring me a goddamn ghost now!"* I yelled at the storm, as if our youth could accomplish even this, the raising of the dead.

v.

One vacation, I stayed at a hotel that had once been a castle and a country house. The proprietor took pity on me, or, more likely, on my parents, who couldn't afford to fly me home for so short a time, and who were frantic with worry as to where I'd go. He only charged me thirteen pounds a night to stay. He was a genial, kind man who claimed to be related to the astronomer Ptolemy.

The castle keep and dungeon were supposedly haunted. He took his guests on a tour. He showed us the parapet where a young maid had leaped to her death rather than marry a cad. "And on the spot where she fell," he said mysteriously, "no grass will grow."

I looked down over the wall.

"Hey," I said. "It's paved."

"There's no grass, though," he said. "See? No grass?"

The previous year on Halloween, the owner of the place had invited an American psychic to come and see if there were any presences in the hotel. She determined, of course, that the place was completely crammed with presences; they were all up and down the staircase; they were stacked like mugs; they peered out from each other's bellies.

I spent the days of that week walking alone in the woods or riding my bike through the flat fields down to the sea. It was strange, for the first time in my life, to be in a place where no one could know me. I was three thousand miles from home, three thousand miles from the cul de sacs and woodchip plantings and cowprint valances of my suburban town. I didn't have to be anyone. I could be whoever I wanted. I walked on old logging trails through the pine woods.

And I used the time alone to remake who I was. When I went into town, I visited used clothing shops and bought old clothes. I remade my wardrobe. I bought waistcoats—which is what they called vests—and neckties, and starched collars of stiff cloth or celluloid; I found a few old tweed suits for ten or fifteen pounds (about twenty dollars) at market stalls. I learned how to attach collars with studs. I put away my orange-stitched jeans, my eighties Izod shirts, my threadbare purple cords. My glasses now were horn-rimmed. I was a new man.

In these clothes, I haunted the woods.

I ate lunch usually in a nearby pub, where they referred to me as "The Vicar," evidently because I looked somber and I always dressed too formally. One day I asked the regulars about the ghost up in the castle. Many of them had mothers or sisters who had worked on the staff there. One told how his mother, who was making the beds in one of the bedrooms, stepped out onto the balcony for a moment and felt the French windows slam shut behind her. She was trapped. She shimmied along to the next balcony and found her way in. She called some of the other maids upstairs. When they got back to the room she had been cleaning, it was locked from the inside. Forcing the door, they found the room in disarray. Someone had torn the sheets off the bed, rumpled everything, thrown objects around on the tables.

For All Hallows' Eve, the hotel had a dinner for their guests in the great hall of the keep. It was a wonderful dinner. Some carrot bisque I really could go for now. On the wall, there was a mummified cat in a case. It had been drained of all its fluids some centuries before.

I sat next to a witty woman in her fifties or sixties from Connecticut. We had a lively and flirtatious conversation. Finally, talk came around to the ghost. I was skeptical. I pointed out that there were flagstones where the maiden fell. Nothing could grow there but lichen.

"Did you see . . ." I whispered, smirking. "Last year they had some kind of psychic come."

"Oh, I know. Please," she said, shaking her head with a little smile. "And they say all the usual things about people seeing shapes, you know, at midnight."

"Yes—always midnight. This is what I'm wondering: Do ghosts observe daylight saving time? Do they set their clocks back? Or half the year, do they appear accidentally at eleven?"

She laughed. "I have a secret," she said.

"And leap year," I continued. "I guess they figure that in, too."

She admitted, "I played the psychic."

"What?" I stopped and squinted. "Were you just acting?"

She smiled. "They wanted a psychic, and I agreed to be one."

"But did you feel something there?" I asked.

She shrugged. "I gave them a good line about Presences."

"See?" I said, pointing. "That's what I thought. There's nothing."

She looked at me strangely. "You're young," she said. "I was the one actually playing the role—I was the one making it all up—but that's why I believe it now."

vi.

The Marquis of Hartington relates that, as a boy, he once met a phantom monk on a staircase. At Renishaw, seat of the Sitwells—a family of writers, aesthetes, and poets who, at parties, would recite nonsense verse while hidden behind a screen—at

Renishaw, in the night, some unseen Thing was known to plant three kisses with lips as cold as ham on the cheeks of virgin girls. Raynham Hall had a specter who walked the corridors at midnight. Captain Marryat, author of swashbuckling nautical tales, one night shot at it in his underwear.

vii.

When I was done with my year in England, I came back to go to college in the States. It did not go well. Nothing seemed real. Sure, my roommates and I attempted Halloween rituals—we dressed in robes and went out into the quadrangle and sacrificed a pizza by stapling it to a tree—but somehow it was not the same. I couldn't sleep. I spent the nights wandering around the city. Nothing seemed right. Finally, my father pointed out to me gently that I was wasting his money, and suggested that I drop out at the end of the term. It was good advice. I dropped out.

I no longer felt at home in my own country. Perhaps I never had been. Perhaps that was why I had chosen to go to England in the first place.

Nothing seemed as real to me as what had happened there.

It took several months for me to realize the dolorous, stupid predicament I had gotten myself into: Nothing seemed like living unless it was like something that I had read in a book.

This is what my fascination with England amounted to. I was only inhabiting my own life fully when I was surrounded by the trappings of someone else's fiction.

Others lived that way too. Most people did. College, for example, was a particular narrative—something from *Animal House* or *Porky's*, or even *Porky's II*. That was fun to watch, but those were not my stories.

After I dropped out of college, I worked at a department store. We were two floors underground, beneath a luxury hotel.

None of us who worked there was particularly happy. We watched college kids come down with their parents and buy things. They all had platinum cards. One day, we had the woman from the print department wrap us up for shipping.

This was funny at first, but the packing tape got in our hair.

We sat there, in our boxes, looking up at the ceiling.

"It's these lights," said my friend Bill.

"What?" I said.

"It's not real light. You can tell. They flicker. It's like phantom light. Ghost bulbs." He sighed, and shifted in his crate. "That's how fluorescents work. You can tell we're all really sitting here underground in the dark, in a cave." He pulled his hand out of the tape and held it in front of my face. He said, "We're just seeing the illusion of light."

viii.

A year later, I went back to college in England. It worked out well. On a practical, educational level, I loved the intellectual brutality of the system there— when I didn't work, I was found out and slammed—but equally important, there were more of the inevitable, absurd images that I needed to digest to confirm that I really was living: the ancient stone courtyards, the Gothic chapels, the people in black gowns. We got drunk, like other undergraduates, but we did it wearing tuxedos, in antique paneled rooms, so it seemed different, somehow. It was the end of the 1980s, an age when greed and capital seemed entertaining. Margaret Thatcher was Prime Minister of England.

But it was not just a country of cobbled passages and physicists biking beneath the lindens. There had been race riots in London. The cities in the north were crumbling. Men and women were dying in the struggle for Irish independence. I had learned while there about how the British were marked for life by their accent, which revealed region and economic class; and for the first time, I discovered hints that America itself might have a class system, though we struggled hard to hide it.

I did not pay much attention to these things, however. We all were safely tucked away in cloisters. I read Shakespeare and Milton, Jane Austen and Evelyn Waugh, and the tale of Sir Gawain and the Green Knight. I learned how to serve off a platter with one hand.

The university was full of ghosts. Not only the ones who were supposed to linger in certain chambers, weeping for strange sins—but also the ghosts of those we learned about, the constant presence of the dead— Christopher Marlowe the murdered playwright, Alfred Lord Tennyson and his dead friend Hallam, John Maynard Keynes and his economics, Byron with his dancing bear, kings and princes and ostlers and serving maids, and farmers who brought their goods across the fens. They were still there, standing over our shoulders. We always had to account for them in conversation, as a cup is set out for Elijah at the seder meal.

ix.

It is said that in Cambridge at Girton College, a dead girl in white walks one of the staircases. A man in a gown, with a hole in his face, wanders the streets. Emmanuel College is haunted by a squat, dead bride in a gray veil. At Peterhouse, a spirit knocks on windows near a cramped and weedy graveyard. The haunting of Corpus Christi College became so troublesome that the undergraduates arranged for an exorcism. It was not particularly successful. The ghost got angry and attacked an atheist. Following this, the college threw up its hands and gave the haunted rooms to an American, who was apparently sufficiently banal to banish the spirit forever. At least, it has not been seen since.

x.

I considered staying in England forever. I applied to do graduate research on Renaissance poetry at Oxford, and got in. I don't know when I started to go sour on the idea.

One evening in my final year, I was at a party. It was a drinks party held in someone's room on one of the old courts. The two guys who were holding the party had met each other and become friends at a previous party when one of them had hired the other to stand still, dressed in a toga, bearing a flaming torch.

They were telling me about the ghost in their rooms.

"We made some inquiries through a Ouija board," said one.

"The board was missing its planchette," said the other. "We used a shot glass."

"You will be terrified."

"There was a boy."

"He died of consumption."

"He was calling out. Through the board."

"For what, one might ask? One doesn't know."

"A consumptive boy. Very feeble."

"Poor speller."

"Lackadaisical in his use of vowels."

My friend Alec had just come in, looking anxiously around the party. He waved to me, and began working his way over. He called out to me, "Yankee! Hey,

Yank!" The room was candlelit. The stereo was playing an old LP of Corelli concerti.

The two hosts were still talking about their consumptive specter.

"One is now too terrified to sleep here."

"One must put on soothing music."

Alec reached us. He grabbed my arm. "Hey,
Yankee," he said, over the talking, over the music of
the strings, through the antique candlelight, "Yank—
Saddam Hussein didn't agree to the U.S. demands."

"Pardon?" I said.

I looked around the room—as if waking—at the
blazers, the black dresses, the ties, the wobbling
phonograph arm on the record of Corelli.

"Iraq," Alec said. "You've just started to bomb
Iraq."

xi.

The peculiarity of the juxtaposition startled me.

I walked home that night after the party through the
drizzle and the murky blur of ornamental gatehouses.

I was tired of the rain, tired of the courtyards and
the cloisters.

I looked around the deserted streets.

And I started to see, by the fact that I was in a land
which seemed so familiar, and yet which was so alien,
that my nation and I were part of a world I did not
understand. The Cold War had ended, and the Berlin

Wall had just come down. We did not live outside of time. History was not a pageant, the dead trooping and arrayed for our delectation; history was still moving. Bombers were flying over the desert. While I strolled up King's Parade, three CNN reporters— named Arnett, Shaw, and Holliman—jabbered, trapped in their Baghdad hotel room, shouting out descriptions of what they saw while the muffled thud of detonations echoed in the background. I had stood in cobbled courtyards and talked with friends about how Chinese students had been gunned down by their own government, half a world away, in Tiananmen Square. No, history was not just for the dead.

I was sick of cloisters and courtyards.

It was time to go home.

xii.

The ancient rules of myth demand that a traveler must leave home to grow—must go out and attain some ordained thing in a strange and holy Otherworld before returning changed and wiser. But it is not that simple, of course, because once you have left home, it isn't quite home anymore when you return.

I returned to America, which was what I thought of as "the real world." It was an inauspicious return. Somehow, there didn't seem to be many employment opportunities for a *fin de siècle* dandy anymore.

I applied unsuccessfully for a few jobs, and then,

having no real skills or prospects, I went back to work at the department store.

I worked there for some years, re-stocking CDs, alphabetizing. Every morning I rode the train reading Restoration comedy, and at lunchtime I read Dante in the food court at a Sbarro's.

My parents had taken out a second mortgage on our house to pay for my education. They no longer owned the place they lived. For this, they got back a son who smirked at them and thought they were dull because they had no enthusiasm for the harpsichord.

I had returned to America because I believed that it would be a return to simplicity, and that simplicity was virtuous and true. And yes, my world no longer smacked of effete over-sophistication—I no longer heard news of momentous events while discussing ghosts at midnight in candlelit rooms with Corelli playing in the background. But nothing was more real in America. It was no more virtuous, no less irrelevant and absurd to hear news with Paula Abdul or C+C Music Factory rocking in the background, with our faces lit in the glow of David Letterman's gappy midnight grin.

Nothing seemed real. It seemed like everyone around me was waiting for their *real* life start.

Occasionally, I would sit on the Boston wharves in the evening and look out toward England, where my friends were attending parties, and writing books and speeches. Looking east, I could see a ghost of who I could have been—a life I had turned down to come back to pizza and minimum wage.

I watched the horizon.

I could see my spirit glimmer there and wince at the sight of me and kick the sand along his native shore.

xiii.

It has been many years since all of this happened, and I do not think about England much anymore. It seems like an unreal time, and the places I lived seem like unreal places. When I picture myself as a teenager, as a younger man—emaciated, dressed in starched collars and a tie—I can only picture myself as a kind of weird insect, a twiggy thing with chiton.

On occasion, once or twice a year, I will think of the friends I have forgotten, and I will feel the tug of my ghost overseas.

Of course, we are all awash in ghosts—ghosts of who we've been, or what we might have been, or who we are.

But I think of those times when I was sitting on the docks in Boston, looking toward England; what worried me as I sat there was not, perhaps, that there was a spirit left behind in England, my abandoned replica, wandering free of my body. On the contrary, I worried that, by coming back, I was not the one who had chosen the real world. I worried that maybe I had made a terrible mistake, and that I was the one who was the ghost. That this was not a life. That I did not return to this country at all, but just sent back a specter to America to perform a few hollow deeds, and that the specter was me.

I looked around me at others who walked through the city, and I saw that many had the same quality of exile, even when they were at home. Some longed for a time; some for a person; some for a place. I saw that people who passed through the streets with me or worked in the department store or talked near me on the subway could not shake off a fear that they did not inhabit their own lives.

Though I have forgotten England, I have not forgotten the ghosts.

We touch ourselves and expect our hands to pass through our chests. Our bodies go off together to conferences and boxing matches. We wander and make frantic phone calls in search of them. We hope that someone has caught a glimpse of us.

Look at those around you. Ask yourself if they are solid or if they are trapped between worlds, compelled flickering to act a life that is no longer theirs. There are many who never feel that they will ever be at rest, or ever be at home.

This is why the world is haunted. This accounts for its sense of terror, and also its infinite possibility.

m. t. anderson

M. T. ANDERSON studied English literature at Harvard and Cambridge universities. After graduating, he spent some years working at a department store and later got a job as an editorial assistant at a publishing house. Eventually, he went back to school and received an MFA in Creative Writing from Syracuse University. He is currently on the faculty of Vermont College's MFA Program in Writing for Children.

M. T. Anderson has written three novels for young adults—*Thirsty* (1997), *Burger Wuss* (1999), and *Feed* (2002), the last of which was a finalist for the National Book Award and the winner of the 2002 *Los Angeles Times* Book Prize. He has written two picture book biographies of classical composers, the most recent being *Strange Mr. Satie* (2003).

"Going overseas to live for a while when you're young is a great idea," he says. "It's important that we all learn to look at our own culture and our own home from the outside, however uncomfortable that may be. Sometimes when you're too much a part of something, you can't see it clearly. If you don't ever leave home, you can't ever return."

This is me in Hollywood, California, at the apex of my career as a song writer/musician. The year was 1972, just before I went off to study in Bergamo, Italy.

ahoy, down there!
by GRAHAM SALISBURY

IT'S DUSK ON the waterfront in Venice.

I feel a bit bewildered, but happily so, under this moody, slate-colored sky. The sun is a red so deep I can stare right at it as it slips into the purple-black clouds way out on the horizon. Just across the water, the island of San Giorgio Maggiore sits like an emperor on a throne, staff in hand, still and stately.

I'm scrunched-up-like, hugging myself, as if I were cold. But the warmth of the day still lingers in the low concrete wall I'm sitting on.

No, it's not cold.

Still, my arms are crossed, shoulders close.

At first I thought it was the sea causing me to turtle in like this, or the red sun wobbling on its surface. Or maybe it was the dreamy thoughts I've been having lately. But no, it's not that. The poetry of this land would be breathtaking to any stranger.

No.

It's that small piece of cloth.

No question.

I didn't expect this.

✴ ✴ ✴ ✴

I'm a few days shy of eight months living and studying in Bergamo, Italy, a place so old it creaks in the wind. I came here fresh out of college to study in an elementary-level Montessori teaching program. There are students here from all over the world. Our classes are taught in Italian, by a man and woman one degree removed from Maria Montessori herself. The lessons are translated into English by a young woman from Mexico. I've been working hard. I know my stuff.

But this is the weekend, *fine settimana*.

And I am away.

✴ ✴ ✴ ✴

Two weeks ago I took a train down along the upper curve of the western coast. I got off in Genoa, wandered around with my orange backpack slung over one shoulder, found a cheap hotel. My intention, as always on these weekend escapes, was to get away from school. See Italy. Absorb the land, listen to the language. Alone.

I like it that way.

Early the next morning as I headed down to the rocky beach waterfront, I stumbled upon a plaque on the side of an old stone building. What I read took a moment to register.

Christopher Columbus's childhood house.

What!

His *house*? Where he actually lived?

It was stony and small and unremarkable. Except that it was built before the U.S.A. was the U.S.A. Except that I, a mildly dim-witted American, had given very little thought to the history beneath my feet. What a twit.

His *house*?

In Bergamo, my school is in a building that was built in the 1300s. I thought, hey, that's *before* Columbus.

And only *now* that's registering?

Jeez.

❊ ❊ ❊ ❊

Italians don't talk to me much. Oh, they do when I struggle with the language, but mostly it's to relieve their impatience. They're busy people. Have lives to live, things to do, places to go.

But one day while exploring the city of Bergamo, I run across two guys who want to chat.

They are in uniform. Carabinieri, kind of like policemen. Both of them are red-faced and totally plastered.

They know I'm a foreigner by my camera, I suppose. But they think I'm German. Italians are not fond of Germans, which, I am told, has to do with tourism. The "ugly Americans" of Europe.

Anyway, these two drunk cops stagger toward me. I think, ho, these bozos are going to roll me. But they are anything but belligerent.

We talk, or try to.

"*Tedesco*," one of them says.

"No, no," I say quickly. "*Sono Americano.*"

"*Ah, Americano, bene, bene. Donna Summer,*" he says, bouncing to the American music in his head.

"Huh?"

See, the thing is, all these guys want is for me to take their picture. And I'm thinking they want my money. Is this an American thought?

"You *fotografia* . . . mail us it," the music guy says.

"Sure . . . I mean, *va bene, una fotografia, sì, sì.*"

They hold onto each other, grinning like idiots.

They thank me profusely, shaking my hand over and over. I watch them stagger away with their arms across each other's shoulders, singing and waving at the people they pass. Friends.

I think, *Now where in the world am I supposed to send that shot?* I laugh. Those dudes are zonkered.

And then I am alone again.

✳ ✳ ✳ ✳

Italians are kind of quirky, too.

Like at the bank. You see, they're not keen on the order of lines. They like to bunch up and squeeze in and nudge their way to the teller. It's disconcerting to be in the middle of it, pressed up against people I don't know like that. But I've gotten used to it. Actually, I think it's funny.

I especially enjoy the clerks in the back, behind the tellers. Men, mostly. Dang near every one of them is a hunt-and-peck typist. And often they peck with a cigarette between their fingers. It's hilarious. Like comic-book characters.

∗ ∗ ∗ ∗

This country is spooky, too.

A while back, I'm standing at an *edicola* buying a magazine called *Topolino*, which is an Italian Mickey Mouse comic-book thing the size and shape of an issue of *Reader's Digest*. It's what I read to practice the language. It helps. Really. "*Ohh, sto male lo stomaco,*" Topolino says, holding his gut.

"*Mi piace Topolino,*" I say to *la signora*. I grin and hold up the latest edition.

But she's looking beyond me, at a massive troop of army-looking guys. They are marching toward us, crowding people and cars off the street. It's sort of like a parade, only it's not. It's a show of power—khaki uniforms with bands of red, and faces so grim they could stop a freight train.

"*Mi scusi, signora, ma . . . chi sono . . . ?*"

La signora steps back into the shadows of the newsstand. Her eyes dart away from mine. "*Comunisti,*" she whispers, then hides completely.

I turn back to the street. Communists?

Three, four, five hundred of them. They all look the same, with the same purpose in their eyes. They don't glance at me or anyone else, as if they're all hypnotized.

After they pass, *la signora* steps back into the light, scowling after them.

"Huh . . . *Comunisti,*" I mumble to myself.

La signora gives me this look that says Time to move on, *Americano,* as if my being there too long is causing some unseen eyebrow to raise.

✶ ✶ ✶ ✶

Italy is beautiful, too.

Especially the girls. *Le ragazze.*

Ho!

I can't help but gawk at them in their spray-on jeans, so tight I can't imagine how they might have gotten them on. They sit around in the piazzas, so stunning.

And so utterly inaccessible.

But actually, the most beautiful sight I ever saw, even to this day, was in the Basilica of St. Peter in la Città del Vaticano, in Roma. It is Michelangelo's *Pietà,* created in 1499, when he was twenty-four years old— a heartbroken Mother Mary holding her destroyed son across her lap, so staggeringly beautiful to me I ached to share my feelings with someone. Anyone.

But I was alone.

⚹ ⚹ ⚹ ⚹

Today I am on the waterfront in Venezia.

Away, again.

This city is as romantic as you might think. Unlike the people of Bergamo, the people of Venice move in a leisurely way. No cars that I can see. Waterways are its streets. Gondolas are its taxis. Duomos, piazzas, a few thousand birds. Cramped brick alleyways with cats sitting on windowsills. Pocket-sized shops and immaculately dressed Venetians, who speak an incomprehensible dialect.

And, of course, there's the ocean.

I stop at the Ponte dei Sospiri, where doomed convicts once gazed out at the world as they crossed from the court to prison, the sparkling canal beneath them. I try to imagine having been one of them.

"Ahoy, down there."

I look up, suddenly. That's English, American English. I turn to see where it's coming from.

"I said, *Ahoy*, down there!"

"Shaddup!" someone shouts back.

There. . . . Look!

Ho!

How come I hadn't noticed it before? It's right there, you dingbat, just down the promenade. An

American destroyer, the size of three city blocks, gray and spiked with antennas and cannons that poke up and out like stubby centipede legs.

And on the stern, on a flagstaff, the ensign of freedom. That small piece of cloth.

Bright, clean, snappy.

It flaps lightly in the breeze coming in off the *laguna*.

I gawk. It's been eight months since I've seen an American flag.

My flag.

My throat is tight. It burns, and memories of people and old attachments rise up inside me, running wild, dancing, hugging, singing, laughing. I see all the places I've been and loved and become a part of—Kailua-Kona, Kamuela, Hilo, Honolulu, Lahaina, Kaneohe, Kailua, Los Angeles, Santa Barbara.

My God, how I love the sight of that flag.

I creep closer to the battleship, berthed alongside the promenade Riva degli Schiavoni, in Venice at dusk—right here, so far from home.

I get right up next to it, study its taut dock lines, breathe the diesely air, listen to bilge water gurgling into the sea from a stained portal.

There is a sailor hanging over the side on a small wooden seat, a can of paint snug beside him. He's sanding a rusty spot on the hull.

Shhh, shhh, shhh, shhh.

Scraping, scraping.

Shhh, shhh, shhh, shhh.

Sanding the hull.

All I hear is the scraping. Rust off metal.

When he's done, he sticks the sandpaper in his pocket and pries the can of paint open with a pocket knife.

He paints battleship gray over the rusty spot. Gray over rust. Gray over rust.

When he runs out of paint, he glances up.

High above, another sailor leans on his arms out over the gunwale, looking down with the white slash of a cigarette dangling from the corner of his mouth.

The sailor with the paintbrush shouts up at him. "Send down some more (bad word) paint, you (nasty word) lazy (insulting word). Better yet, why don't you come do this (horrid word) job? This (truly nasty almost as bad as you can get word) sucks."

My mouth hangs open. I'm stunned, listening to the beautiful sounds of home.

My eyes fill with water.

Dang.

⊁ ⊁ ⊁ ⊁

Which is why I'm all scrunched up hugging myself.

"Hey, slimeball, where's the (utterly disgusting word) paint!"

Ah, the good old U.S.A.

I love you.

Keep the porch light on. I'm coming home soon.

graham salisbury

GRAHAM SALISBURY'S life would make for fascinating nonfiction: his rock-and-roll band, The Millennium, had a number one hit in the Philippines; he didn't wear shoes until he was in the sixth grade; and he once surfed with a shark. Fortunately for readers, his fiction is equally captivating. A winner of the *Boston Globe-Horn Book* Award, the Scott O'Dell Award for historical fiction, the California Young Reader Medal, and the PEN/Norma Klein award, among other honors, Salisbury has written works including *Blue Skin of the Sea* (1992), *Under the Blood-Red Sun* (1994), *Shark Bait* (1997), *Jungle Dogs* (1998), *Lord of the Deep* (2001), and *Island Boyz* (2002).

Graham Salisbury, who grew up in Hawaii, comes from a hundred-year line of newspapermen, all connected to Hawaii's morning paper, the *Honolulu Advertiser*. But Salisbury chose fiction over journalism. "There's magic in fiction," he says, "and times when completely unexpected things take place as my fingertips walk the keyboard."

Writing "Ahoy, Down There," Salisbury says, "was one of those magic moments where I set out simply to write about a year living in Italy . . . and ended up rekindling my deep and enduring love for the magnificent country I live in."

A graduate of California State University, Salisbury received an M.F.A. from Vermont College of Norwich University. He lives with his family in Portland, Oregon. You can visit him on his website, at www.grahamsalisbury.com.

Here I am on the Yangtze river in 1922.

mk
by JEAN FRITZ

I ALWAYS DISLIKED being called an MK or a PK, although I was both—a Missionary Kid and a Preacher's Kid. I heard this most often in China where I grew up, even though China was swarming with MKs. Actually, many MKs simply basked in their MKness. Not me. Calling me an MK just boxed me in, telling me who I was while I was still trying to figure it out for myself. I never knew an MK to follow in his father's footsteps and become an M, but most of us understood that if it weren't for our fathers' commitment, we wouldn't even be in China. And we knew that our lives would forever be colored by our China childhoods. Indeed, although we didn't realize it yet, we shared a common quest. Where did we belong? How were we to find a commitment strong enough to direct us? How was China itself shaping us?

Those early years were filled with pictures that were distinctly Chinese. Village life was lived in poverty and in the open. Everyday functions—eating, often urinating, occasionally death, scolding, ordering, endless backbreaking work—were all right before our eyes. Every emotion of the human spirit, every trial was amplified, played out in public.

I remember lying awake in my bed, listening to a woman in the Chinese community behind us. Every night she would come out of her house and begin screaming abuse at everyone in her family, at her neighbors, at the world itself. It was as if she were uncorking a bottle of pent-up rage and letting it loose into the night. To my amazement, her voice never gave out; it just became shriller. To me, she became one of the voices of China, enduring like other snapshots, desolate, without hope.

China revealed itself in unexpected but unforgettable moments. Once when I was in a ricksha, a policeman diverted traffic, including me, around an obstacle in the road. A large umbrella was open, its handle stuck in the dirt. Under the umbrella lay a dead man. Had he not been able to make it to the other side? Had he just toppled over? I wondered. Wonder seemed to lie at the heart of my childhood.

Yet basically there was always a deep sense of peace in China. It had to do with time—not minutes, months, or years, but time as a whole, the foreverness of it. Living beside the Yangtze River as I did, I could feel the full of time gathered up in the river, brown with age, flowing all the way back to the Beginning. Its smell, containing centuries, came up from the dankest bottom. In my mind I held together the river and a temple that stood nearby and that I could always hear even if I couldn't see it. Outside the front door of the temple there dangled a huge brass gong with a monk in close attendance beside it. At regular intervals the monk struck the gong. The ring would resound in the valley until it had almost faded away.

Then the monk would strike again. Sometimes another monk would relieve him, striking at just the right moment, so that the gong became a living thing for those who could hear, a reminder that time was going on and on just as it always had. Although I'm sure that gong no longer accompanies life along the Yangtze, I still hear its echo, which only shows how far China has reached into my soul.

I suspect for most of us MKs China not only sharpened our sense of time but our sense of place. We always knew where we were in relation to the rest of the world. And we noticed. Perhaps because we knew we would be leaving China sometime (we wouldn't be MKs or even Ks forever), we developed the habit of observing our surroundings with care. We have strong memories, which explains why as an adult, walking along a beach in Maine, I suddenly found myself on the verge of tears. In front of me, pushing up from the crevice of a rock, was a wild bluebell like the wild bluebells I had known in my summers at Kuling. Suddenly I was a child again. I was back in China, welcoming bluebells back in my life.

For a long time it was hard for me to unscramble the strings that made up my quest. I have noticed, however, that those MKs who were born in China and stayed there through their high school years were more likely to commit their lives in some way to China. After finishing their higher education in the States, they would return to China as consuls, as teachers, as businessmen and women, as writers, as historians.

I wouldn't be staying through high school. My family planned to return to America when I had finished seventh grade, whether I was finished with China or not. Of course I knew I had to become an American, the sooner the better. So far away from America, I didn't feel like a real American. Nor would I, I thought, until I had put my feet down on American soil.

I had just finished sixth grade at the British School

in Wuhan, so I would have one more year to go. Nothing would change that. I knew that there was fighting up and down the Yangtze River, but the Chinese were always fighting—warlord against warlord. That had nothing to do with me. But as soon as I saw the servant from next door racing toward our house with a message for my mother, I knew something was happening. Since we had no phone, we depended on our German neighbors for emergency messages. My father had called, the servant explained. All American women and children had to catch the afternoon boat to Shanghai. The army, which had done so much damage to Nanjing (just down the river), was on its way here.

As I helped my mother pack, my knees were shaking. I had only felt this once before. My mother and I had been in a ricksha on the way to the racecourse when farmers ran to the road, calling hateful words at us and throwing stones. The ricksha-pullers were fast runners, so we weren't hurt, but I told myself this was like Stephen in the Bible who was stoned to death. He just didn't have a ricksha handy. By the time we reached the boat that afternoon, my knees were normal. So was I. And I knew what our plans were. My father and other American men would work in the daytime, but for safety at night they would board one of the gunboats anchored in the river. The women and children going to Shanghai would be protected from bullets by steel barriers erected around the deck. And when we reached Shanghai, then what? I asked my mother.

We would be staying with the Barretts, another missionary family, who had one son, Fletcher, who was two years younger than I and generally unlikable. Mr. Barrett met us in Shanghai and drove us to their home, where his wife was on the front porch. My mother greeted her warmly but I just held out my hand and said, "Hello, Mrs. Barrett," which I thought was adequate. She raised her eyebrows. "Have you become so grown up, Jean," she said, "that I'm no longer your 'Auntie Barrett'?"

I didn't say that I'd always been too grown up for the "auntie" business. I just smiled. In China all MKs called their parents' friends "auntie" or "uncle." Not me. Mrs. B. pushed Fletcher forward.

"Fletcher has been so excited about your visit, Jean," she said. "He has lots of games to show you. Now, run along, children."

Fletcher did have a lot of games. He decided what we'd play—rummy, then patience, while he talked a blue streak. I didn't pay much attention until, in the middle of an Uncle Wiggley game, he asked me a question.

"Have you ever been in love, Jean?" he asked.

What did he think I was? I was twelve years old, for heaven's sakes!

Ever since first grade I'd been in love with some-one. The boys never knew it, of course.

Fletcher hadn't finished with love. "I'm in love now," he said. "I'll give you a hint. She's an MK."

"Naturally."

"And she's pretty." Then he suddenly shrieked out the answer as if he couldn't contain it a second longer. "It's you," he cried. "Y-O-U."

Well, Fletcher Barrett was even dumber than I'd thought. No one had ever called me "pretty" before. Not even my parents. Besides, this conversation was making me sick. "I'm tired," I said. "I think I'll get my book and lie down."

At the last minute I had slipped my favorite book in my suitcase. It was one my father and I had read last year—*The Courtship of Miles Standish*—all about the first settlers in America. I knew them pretty well now and often visited with Priscilla Alden.

Settled on the bed in the room I'd been told was mine, I opened the book and let the Pilgrims step off the *Mayflower* into Shanghai. Priscilla was one of the first.

"You're still a long way from Plymouth," I told her, "but you'll get there. Think you'll like it?"

"I know I will," she answered promptly. "Every-thing will be better there."

"How do you know?"

"It's a new country. It will be whatever we make it."

"It may be hard," I warned her.

"Maybe," she admitted. "But I'll never give up. Neither will John," she added.

I was being called for supper. I waited for the Pilgrims to get back on the *Mayflower*. Then I closed the book and went downstairs.

The days that followed, I spent mostly with Fletcher, whether I liked it or not. Fletcher was fussing now that the summer was almost over and he'd have to go back to school soon.

"I thought you'd like it," I said. "After all, it's an American school and you're an American."

"So what?"

"Don't you feel like an American when you're in school?"

"What's there to feel?"

He was impossible. If he had gone to a British school, the way I had all my life, he might realize how lucky he was. The Shanghai American School was famous. Children from all over China were sent there to be boarders. Living in Shanghai, Fletcher was just a day student. But even so!

Then one day my mother got a letter from my father. The danger was mostly over, he thought, but some foreign businesses were not reopening. The British School had closed down. (Good news!)

The Yangtze River boats went back in service the next week, so my mother went downtown to buy our tickets back to Wuhan. Fletcher was back in school now, and as soon as he came home, he rushed to see me, his face full of news.

"Your mother is only buying one ticket," he informed me. "You're not going. You're going to the Shanghai American School as a boarder."

"My mother would never do that. You're crazy," I replied. "Where did you get such an idea?"

"I overheard our mothers talking. It's true, Jean."

"Yeah, like cows fly."

When my mother came back, I could see that she was upset. Fletcher did a disappearing act; I figured he didn't want to be caught in a lie.

"Oh, I'm sorry, Jean," my mother said, her eyes filling with tears. She put her arms around me. "Since the British School is closed," she said, "I've arranged for you to be a boarder at the American School. It won't be for long. We may even go back to America early. At least I'll know you're safe."

I knew my mother was worried that I'd be homesick, so I couldn't let on how I really felt. (Just think, I told myself, I'd have almost a year to practice being an American.) I buried my head on her shoulder. "I'll be okay," I said, sniffing back fake tears. Sometimes it's necessary to deceive your parents if you love them, and I did love mine.

After my mother left on the boat, Mr. Barrett took me to the Shanghai American School (SAS for short). I guess I expected some kind of immediate transformation. I always felt a tingling when I saw the American flag flying over the American consulate. Surely it would be more than a tingling now; surely it would overwhelm me. But when we went through the iron gates of the school grounds, I didn't feel a thing. On the football field a group of high school girls were practicing cheerleading. They were jumping, standing on their hands, yelling rah, rah, rah. It just seemed like a lot of fuss about football. What was the matter with me?

The dormitory where I'd be living was divided in half by a swinging door. The high school girls were on one side of the door; the junior high (which included me) were on the other. On my side there were two Russian girls and two American MKs, the Johnson sisters, who had long hair braided and wound around their heads like Sunday school teachers. And there was Paula, my American roommate, who looked as though she belonged on the other side of the door. Hanging in our shared closet I noticed a black velvet dress. And a pair of high heeled shoes. She wore them to tea dances, she explained, when one of her brother's friends came to town. She was squinting her eyes as she looked at me, sizing up my straight hair and bangs.

"I happen to know you're an MK," she said, "but you don't have to look like one." The latest style in the States, she told me, was a boyish bob. She'd give me one, she decided.

So that night she put a towel around my shoulders and newspaper on the floor, and she began cutting. This might make all the difference, I thought, as I watched my hair travel to the floor.

It didn't. My ears might have felt more American, but not me. After being in hiding all their lives, my ears were suddenly outdoors, looking like jug handles on each side of my face. I'd get used to them, I told myself. Meanwhile I had to admit that SAS was a big improvement over the British School. Even without an American flag feeling, I enjoyed the months I was there.

What I enjoyed most were the dances, except they weren't dances. There were too many MKs in the school, and the Ms didn't approve of dancing. Instead, we had "talk parties." The girls were given what looked like dance cards and the boys were supposed to sign up for the talk sessions they wanted. Of course a girl could feel like a wallflower if her card wasn't filled up, but mine usually was. These parties gave me a chance to look over the boys in case I wanted to fall in love, and actually I was almost ready to make a choice when my parents suddenly appeared. It was early spring. Just as my mother had suspected, we were going to America early.

I knew that three weeks crossing the Pacific would be different from five days on the Yangtze but I didn't know how different. My father had given me a gray-

and-green plaid steamer rug that I would put over me when I was lying on my long folding deck chair. At eleven o'clock every morning a waiter would come around with a cup of "beef tea." I loved the idea of drinking beef tea under my steamer rug but it didn't happen often. The captain said this was the roughest crossing he'd ever made, and passengers spent most of their time in their cabins. If they came out for a meal, they were lucky if they could get it down before it came back up again. I had my share of seasickness, so of course I was glad to reach San Francisco.

I couldn't wait to take my first steps on American soil, but I expected the American soil to hold still for me. Instead, it swayed as if we were all still at sea, and I lurched about as I had been doing for the last three weeks. I noticed my parents were having difficulty, too. "Our heads and our legs aren't ready for land," my father explained. "It takes a little while." We spent the night in a hotel and took a train the next day for Pittsburgh where our relatives were meeting us.

It was a three-day trip across most of the continent, but it didn't seem long. Every minute America was under us and rushing past our windows—the Rocky Mountains, the Mississippi river, flat ranch land, small towns, forests, boys dragging school bags over dusty roads. It was all of America at once splashed across where we were, where we'd been, where we were going. How could you not feel American? How could you not feel that you belonged? By the time we were settled at my grandmother's house, I felt as if I'd always been a part of this family. And wasn't it wonderful to have real aunts and uncles, a real grandmother, and yes, even a real bathroom, for heaven's sakes?

I wanted to talk to Priscilla, so I took my book outside, and when I opened it, out tumbled the Pilgrims, Priscilla first. I smiled. Here we were, all of us in America together, and it didn't matter that we came from different times. We all knew that America was still an experiment and perhaps always would be. I was one of the ones who had to try to make the experiment work.

"You'll have disappointments," Priscilla said. "But it will help if you get to know Americans who have spent their lives working on the experiment."

I wasn't sure just what she meant, but I knew it was important. "I'll try," I said.

"Try!" Priscilla scoffed. "If you want to be a real American, you'll have to do more than that." Her voice was fading. Indeed, the Pilgrims themselves were growing faint. Soon they had all slipped away.

I learned about disappointment as soon as I went to school. Of course I was no longer an MK, but I was certainly a curiosity. I was the Kid from China. "Did you live in a mud hut?" one boy asked me. "Did you eat rats and dogs? Did you eat with sticks?"

I decided that American children were ignorant. Didn't their teachers teach them anything? After a while, as soon as anyone even mentioned China, I shut up. "What was the name of your hometown?" I was asked, but I never told. I couldn't bear to have my hometown laughed at.

"Not all American children are ignorant," my mother pointed out. "Just a few who ask dumb questions."

Even in high school, however, I often got the same questions. But now we were studying about the American Revolution and George Washington. Of course I'd always known who Washington was, but knowing history and understanding it are two different things. I had never realized how much he had done to make America into America. No matter how much he was asked to do for his country, he did it, even though he could hardly wait to go back home and be a farmer again. Of course there were disappointments on the way; of course he became discouraged. "If I'd known what I was getting into," he said at the beginning of the Revolution, "I would have chosen to live in an Indian teepee all my life." He never took the easiest way. When he thought his work was over at the end of the Revolution, he agreed to work on the Constitution. When the country needed a president, he took the oath of office. When his term was over, he was persuaded to run once again. Everyone had confidence that as long as he was there, the new government would work.

Although Washington was the first, there were many more like him who were, as Priscilla would say, "real" Americans. As I went through college and read about them, I knew I wanted to write about them someday. I might not talk to them in the same way I talked to Priscilla, but I would try to make them as real as they were when they were alive.

I had the feeling that I was coming to the end of my quest. But not quite. One day when someone asked me where I was born, I found myself smiling. I was for the moment standing beside the Yangtze River. "My hometown," I said, "was Wuhan, China." I discovered that I had to take China with me wherever I went.

jean fritz

A frequent comment about **JEAN FRITZ** is that she makes history fun. But Fritz claims that she just likes a good story and—luckily for readers—she finds lots of them in her historical research. She also notes, "Often I turn up surprises, and of course I pass these on."

Having spent her childhood in China—without setting foot on U.S. soil until she was thirteen—Fritz was determined to learn all she could about America, past and present. This thirst for American history led her to write fresh and entertaining books on such historical figures as George Washington, Harriet Beecher Stowe, Abraham Lincoln, and Lizzie Stanton.

Fritz often visits places connected to her subjects. She went to Italy to celebrate the re-creation of Leonardo da Vinci's monumental bronze horse, the subject of her book *Leonardo's Horse* (2001), and attended a birthday party for Frenchman and Revolutionary War hero Lafayette, the subject of *Why Not, Lafayette?* (1999), in the first town named for him in America: Fayetteville, North Carolina.

Drawing on her own history, Fritz wrote *Homesick* (1982), a Newbery Honor book, about her childhood in China and *China Homecoming* (1985) about going back to China as an adult. When asked whether anything from "MK" has influenced who she is today, Fritz replies, "Once I write about a person or place, I feel that I take possession. Writing this story was one of many steps to make me feel at home in both my countries—China and America. And if the Pilgrims took a place in my real life, it is not surprising. Time has a way of going back and forth when you steep yourself in it."

Jean Fritz has been writing books for over forty years. She currently lives in Dobbs Ferry, New York, on the Hudson River. She has a son, a daughter, and two grandsons.

Above: Here I am with my stepdaughter Jacqui in Leiden, Holland, feeding the geese and trading travel stories. Below: Here's Jacqui hang gliding above Interlaken in the Swiss Alps.

the girl who had no story and had to steal one

by *KATHLEEN KRULL* & *JACQUELINE BREWER*

"CAN YOU STAND some good news? My company is sending me to ITALY for the Bologna Children's Book Fair!!! I'll be there a week. It promises to be tremendously exciting—and also backbreaking work. I still can't believe I'm going to Europe! (And neither can most of the other people in the company.)"

—Kathy Krull, age twenty-seven,
writing to her parents

Yes, my first trip abroad was at the elderly age of twenty-seven. Now I ponder, ever since nosy editor Jill Davis asked me to write a story for this book, just why it took me so long.

After all, as a teen I was a book fiend, and all the best writers traveled. Robert Louis Stevenson, Mark Twain, Jack London, Hemingway and Fitzgerald, and so on . . . where would they be without their travel adventures? Even my heroine Virginia Woolf (of *Mrs. Dalloway* and *A Room of One's Own* fame) informed her writing with firsthand knowledge of the world well outside England. Adventures abroad were required for a writer's life.

Fear and ignorance—these were my two biggest reasons to stay self-contained, or at least within my safe orbit. Smug in my American cocoon, I thought I was Christopher Columbus just going to college in Wisconsin—hey, light years away from Illinois. I was shy and afraid of a lot—talking to strangers, weird foods, crowded places, danger, pain, making mistakes, getting lost, falling ill, you name it. The idea of an organized tour abroad sounded like torture—stuck with people I was sure I wouldn't like—but no way was I brave enough to pull off a trip on my own. The practicalities were way beyond me. How did you know where to go? What did you even pack? And money—the amount needed for a foreign trip seemed insurmountable, and fear made it so.

As an adventurer I was a dud.

Trust me, you don't want to hear the story of my Bologna voyage: there is no story. It was a business trip—on duty from six in the morning to ten at night, scouting new books for our company and selling foreign rights to our books. I barely noticed I was eating the most delicious Italian food of my entire life, that Italian leather shoes were so exquisite (I dashed into a store to buy two pairs), that Italian women (men too—even babies) had such flair and style, that the quality of light on the olive trees . . .

The years buzzed by. I married a travel fiend in California—he had spent his college years vagabonding—and started to roam further afield, and not just for business. My travel was no longer armchair.

One of my stepdaughters, Jacqui Brewer, took after her dad. The very minute she was able to travel, she was gone. At age nineteen, she flew out of San Diego and backpacked through Europe— for *six weeks.* She took in Paris, Amsterdam, Hamburg, Prague, Interlaken, Cinque Terra, Rome, Florence, and Barcelona. Jacqui became my new heroine, and I wanted to learn something from her, put her under a microscope. How was she different from me? What were her secrets? What was her travel adventure story?

Kathleen Krull asks Jacqui Brewer Numerous Nosy Questions

What inspired you to make this trip?

All my life I heard my dad's stories about traveling through Europe—the months he and a buddy toured around in a van they'd bought (meeting great people who became lifelong friends), the year he spent working in an Amsterdam youth hostel, the four months he explored the Greek islands. I suspected travel was in my blood, and it is.

What are the advantages of backpacking and staying in hostels? Wouldn't an organized tour have been a lot easier?

A tour would have taken away the rewards of figuring things out for myself. Doing it yourself teaches real-life skills, like reading maps, and competency with public transportation. And figuring out how to get from here to there is fun. That ended up being where all the laughter and stories were, and all the funky cheap hostels with interesting people.

Weren't you scared?

I found that I got over shyness when I was traveling. I would keep running into the same travelers in other countries, and by that time we were friends. There's so much benefit to being open, breaking out of your shell, stepping out of your comfort zone. I discovered that I want travel to be a part of my life. I loved making games out of figuring out the train schedules, and deciding how to see as many things as possible during a given time. No matter what happens, it's always interesting.

What were some of the best moments of your trip?
A one-day solo hike through Gimmelwald. That's a hard-to-get-to little town in Switzerland. It cost more to get there than I planned, but I'd heard such raves about it. It's amazingly beautiful, not like any other place I've been to, with the houses blending right in, all organic and balanced. Ironically, this could have been the *worst* day of the trip, because as I was walking behind a waterfall I suddenly realized I'd lost all of my money for that day. I was ready to flip out, but some kids at a youth hostel at the edge of a cliff made me dinner and helped me out. It ended up being the *best* day. Then there was the most magical place I stayed—people at the train station in Interlaken recruited us to stay at this hostel called the Funny Farm. It turned out to be a big funky house, brightly painted and full of great people. There were no locks on the doors—everyone operated on trust. One of the few rules was that if you spilled beer some rowdy Australians threw you in the pool at the end of a spiral path. Everyone was always cooking different

things, and I spent nights around a campfire talking with the guys from Australia. My friends and I ended up staying a couple days longer than we planned, and I even went back by myself later in the trip for two more days.

Let's talk money. How did you pull off a trip like this, moneywise?
I was lucky enough that my grandmother gave money to me and my sister for a trip to Europe. I worked hard at summer jobs and saved, plus I had help from various other family members. I tried bargaining with them—if I put in all I can, will they match it, or help with the plane ticket or something else. I put energy into making my arguments as strong as possible—I stressed the importance of travel, how I want to become more self-reliant, and why I should start now. I was also lucky to have a good group of friends who were planning to travel together—I found out I could use that as leverage, to make the trip sound safe to worried adults.

What surprised you most about your journey?
That I was better at being flexible than I thought I would be.

One night, I was alone on a train and I realized it was going in exactly the opposite direction from where I wanted to go. Or rather, I was on the right train but the wrong car—it split off in the wrong direction. I was literally eighteen hours on a train that time, and thirty-six hours late to meet a friend, so I was ready to flip out. Then I realized I was keeping my composure surprisingly well. I found out that staying rational makes all the difference in not being an easy victim of bad things or bad people.

After a while, I started breaking off from my friends more and more and doing more alone. That was the other surprise—how much I embraced traveling alone. Also, being around all these free-floating travelers made me into more of a low-maintenance person, even once I returned to California. Worrying about whether my hair was okay or if I was wearing the same clothes—these dropped way down on my list of priorities. This ended up being a permanent change—being more in the moment.

So what was in your backpack?
Before I left, I was hyperorganized and made numerous lists of what to bring. This was also the subject of endless discussion with my friends. It was summer, so luckily I could travel light with clothes suited for hot weather. Everyone told me not to buy a pack that's too big, and they were right. You're very aware of your backpack, especially when you're trying to get to your hostel—the cheapest ones were usually the longest walks from the train station. Plus stairways—once our

room was up ten flights of stairs. Your pack weighs thirty or forty pounds, depending on whether you're carrying a bottle of wine.

What were the most essential items to pack?
A good pair of running shoes that breathe. I wore the same shoes the entire time. There wasn't really a need for the dressier shoes I brought—I never wore them, even dancing. The shoes got exposed to lots of European water and dirt—even cow patties once, when I was hang gliding through a field of cows. I looked down at my shoes, then decided to worry about it later. For a while they became known as "the poop shoes." Some of my friends had shoes that didn't breathe well, and the stink was a real problem. We would take off our shoes on trains and let them air out in the corridors.

One truly indispensable thing was a package of baby wipes. Running water is not always there when you need it. And a Swiss army knife—I bought mine *in* Switzerland.

What did you wish you had packed?
More summer dresses to dress up quickly and disguise the grunge.

What did you do for food?
We didn't really do any fine dining, and the cheapest food was usually heavy and fried. I set my budget at

fifty dollars a day (not counting the Eurail pass for train travel). I found out some youth hostels were cheaper than I expected, so sometimes I could splurge at restaurants. I'm a vegetarian, so Mediterranean restaurants were my friends, and Spain was tough—they seem to put ham on everything. But eating on the street rather than restaurants was much cheaper and more interesting. I ate tons of falafel. Best of all were simple treats of bread and cheese, with tomatoes you could buy at fruit markets, and maybe a bottle of wine. This made for a great communal meal you could share while relaxing on a park bench. Even Parisians seemed friendly and would call "bon appetit" when they saw us eating like this.

How did you get the information to establish your budget?
Right away I found out certain countries were cheaper than others, so you could try to balance things out. At one point, spending six days in Prague instead of Germany really helped—the hostel in Prague was less than five dollars a night. In Italy, food was inexpensive and excellent, so this made up for the fact that the hostel was surprisingly expensive. Switzerland was the opposite—expensive food, not quite as expensive lodging.

Guidebooks helped (my favorite was *Let's Go*), except that the information dates quickly. Most valuable was word of mouth. I'd meet people on trains—

there's a whole community of fellow travelers, all of them excited to share their well-earned tidbits and secrets. I soaked it all up like a sponge, and by the end of trip people were asking *me* questions. In most countries people sincerely want to help you out— think of how you would help a foreigner traveling in *your* city—it's a natural instinct to help.

What about safety?

I was warned about muggings in my neighborhood in Barcelona, and I did hear screams one night. But the scariest time was that night I went the wrong direction on the train. In general, I had to take care not to arrive in a city by myself late at night—you become an easy target. I found out that if you knew you were going to arrive late, it was a common practice to pass your stop, get a decent night's sleep on the train, and then backtrack the next day. I look what the Spanish call very "rubia"—blonde hair and blue eyes—and so I took more care than usual not to appear too American, to try to blend in.

Why not appear as an American?

I found out you get treated differently if people think you are one. We're seen as obnoxious, arrogant, too interfering with other counties. Everyone does like American movies, but there was a lot of grumbling about McDonald's and other chains. We're seen as always traveling in mobs, speaking English very loud on the trains, spending and eating too much, especially junk food.

A lot of people actually think Americans are idiots. They resent our lack of knowledge about their politics—when they know all about ours. They think we have a basic ignorance of their geography and political leaders. Even our own politics—they think we're not interested in our own leaders. To them we seem well versed in MTV, and just the opposite in global news. One way Americans stand out from other travelers is that they assume that others around them can't understand what they're saying, which can make them look foolish. Actually, most Europeans are multilingual, they understand English perfectly well, and they find this attitude kind of stupid. Some things did make me proud to be American—we're seen as friendly, outgoing people who get out there and will talk to anyone. This contrasts with many countries where people are much more reserved. Also, Americans are seen as motivated, ambitious, and efficient—these are seen as good things, unless you don't like American culture being so prevalent, then it can seem too much.

Aren't you being a little paranoid?
These feelings weren't just a vibe. People would speak ill of Americans right to my face. Sometimes they were astonished to find out I was one. During one interest-

ing talk with an older man in Barcelona, he said, "You're very politically aware for an American."

There's a feeling that we don't appreciate what we have in the United States. Also that religions are so vocal here—they don't understand our abortion politics at all, or why we made such a big deal out of Bill Clinton and Monica Lewinsky. And they resent the idea that we think we can see everything on one trip— "Oh, I've done Europe," after you've been to six or seven cities. It's offensive to them, like we are tourists out to "conquer" Europe.

I have to admit my own attitudes toward Americans changed after this trip—I'm more critical.

I read in the April 8, 2001, New York Times, that even now, 99 percent of college-age kids don't travel abroad—just as I didn't. What would you say to them? My advice is: "Get out!" College kids should look at their options—in California, for example, study-abroad programs are abundant. Don't be scared of money—in general the cost of living is lower abroad. It's not fantastically expensive—it can actually be cheaper, depending where you go.

I read something else interesting in the same article— that, of the kids who do travel abroad, 27 percent go only to English-speaking countries like England and Australia.

Don't be intimidated by a foreign language—just try. Like I said, in most countries people truly want to help you. Plus I've learned that fluency in languages is one of the most valuable skills you can have in the job market *right now*. A language can be much more useful than other courses.

So, how would you sum up your out-of-America story?
It was so eye-opening that I decided right away that I really wanted to try living abroad. As soon as I got back to California, I started finalizing plans to study abroad my senior year, so I could experience living there. Then I changed my major—from Psychology to Global Studies. I felt so connected to the rest of the world. And after being in a place where being multilingual is the norm, I realized the importance of taking more language courses. The trip opened up new options for me and the friends I traveled with and changed our lives in a lot of ways. It planted the seed that we can break boundaries of all kinds. Anything seems possible—what we do with our lives is not limited. I just know my life is going to be interesting.

Thanks, Jacqui, for letting me borrow your story— and for inspiring others who are the RIGHT AGE RIGHT NOW.

kathleen krull

The introduction to **KATHLEEN KRULL**'s Web site, www.kathleenkrull.com, instructs the visitor to "click here if you are nosy." Krull explains, "I'm nosy about people, for example, and the Lives of . . . series allows me to snoop behind the closed doors of some of my favorite groups of (really strange) people."

Many of her books reflect Krull's personal interests: "Nightmares, how fame affects people, World War II and other angles to American History." But her main inspiration is books themselves. Krull explains, "As a child I thought books were the most important thing in the world, and that perception is actually more intense now."

After graduating from Lawrence University in Appleton, Wisconsin, Krull began a career in children's book publishing, working as a children's book editor until she left to become a full-time writer. As well as the Lives of . . . series, Krull has written other biographies including *Harvesting Hope: The Story of Cesar Chavez* (2003) and *Wilma Unlimited: How Wilma Rudolph Became the World's Fastest Woman* (1996) and picture books *Clip Clip Clip: Three Stories about Hair* (2002), illustrated by her husband Paul Brewer, and *M Is for Music* (2003).

She currently lives in San Diego with her husband, children's book illustrator Paul Brewer, and travels abroad frequently, most recently to visit her step-daughter Jacqui Brewer in Leiden, Holland.

Meanwhile, Jacqui Brewer went back to Europe the following year. She traveled throughout Holland, and then to Barcelona, London, Munich, Bruges, Brussels, Galway, Paris, and Copenhagen. In 2002 she graduated with honors in Global Studies from the University of California-Santa Barbara. Currently she is in Southeast Asia, Australia, or South America.

Kathleen Krull's website is www.kathleenkrull.com. (How nosy are you?)